Museums Discovered:
The Calouste Gulbenkian Museum

D0707117

Edited by Eve Sinaiko and Leslie Shore

Editorial Staff: Sandra Moy,
Alison de Lima Greene, and Anthony Strianse

Color photography by Gordon Roberton

Photographs on pages 25, 29, 31, 37, 47, 51, 67,
92, 107, 162, 169-173, 177, and 181 by Renaldo Viegas

Rona Goffen is Professor of Art at
Duke University; Priscilla Soucek is
Hagop Kevorkian Professor of Islamic
Art at the Institute of Fine Arts,
New York University.

Text on pages 152-57 by Leslie Shore;
on pages 192-205 by Eve Sinaiko

ISBN: 0-934516-46-4
Library of Congress Card Catalog Number: 81-71000

Created for Woodbine Books, Inc. by
Shorewood Fine Art Books
475 Tenth Avenue
New York, N.Y. 10018

Thanks are due to Maria Teresa Gomes Ferreira,
Maria Rosa Figueiredo, and Maria Helena Soares Costa
of the Calouste Gulbenkian Museum for their
advice and assistance in the creation of this book.

Museums Discovered: The Calouste Gulbenkian Museum

by Rona Goffen
with a foreword by Maria Teresa Gomes Ferreira
and fifteen essays contributed by Priscilla Soucek

Woodbine Books
Ft. Lauderdale, Florida

Created by Shorewood Fine Art Books
New York

Foreword

The Calouste Gulbenkian Museum was opened on October 2, 1969, fulfilling the wish of its founder to leave his precious art collection to an institution established by his will. It was Gulbenkian's expressed purpose to bring together the work of a lifetime's interest, persistence, and love, and to house it in one place. Since it was specially built for the collection, the museum is, to a certain extent, a reflection of the taste, culture, and spirit of the man who conceived it and brought it about: its intention is, above all, to display works of art for the aesthetic appreciation of the public, and to make them available for study and for the artistic and cultural enrichment of future generations.

The site of the museum in green parkland—the Palhavā Park in Lisbon—creates a sense of tranquility and peace necessary for the contemplation and understanding of works of art in the best possible conditions. Throughout the museum there are innumerable windows opening onto vistas of this park, offering the museum visitor continual contact with nature.

The museum has been designed to retain the intimate quality of Gulbenkian's original private collection, while, at the same time, the arrangement of works follows a chronological and geographical distribution, organized in routes or circuits within the museum as a whole. Thus the visitor can see, on the circuit covering Oriental and Classical art, the galleries dedicated to Egypt, Assyria, and Greece—including an important numismatic collection—Rome, the Islamic East, and the Far East; the second circuit displays European art, with collections of painting, sculpture, ivories and illuminated manuscripts, tapestries and textiles, furniture, gold- and silverware, jewelry, glass, and medallions.

Because the Gulbenkian Museum began as the refined collection of a private connoisseur, it possesses works of great distinction and rarity, even in areas and periods where the holdings are not large. The Egyptian collection, though not extensive, covers most of the historical and artistic periods of this civilization, from the Old Kingdom to the Roman era. The remarkable collection of Greek coins was an area for which the founder had a very particular and constant affection; it is large, and the selection on display in the galleries is of significant stature. A small group of Greek and Roman works of art completes the collection of Classical antiquity, and the culmination of this gallery is a large-scale Oriental bas-relief from the palace of Assurnazirpal at Nimrud.

Perhaps because he was born and lived his early years in Turkey, Gulbenkian had a special interest in the art of the Near and Middle East, particularly that of the time when Islam took root in these regions, with its profound influence on their art. Therefore, the art of Persia, Turkey, Syria, the Caucasus, Armenia, and India, of the period between the Mongol invasions of Genghis Khan and the end of the eighteenth century, is richly documented in the collection. A total of 250 pieces selected for exhibition, with numerous ceramics, rugs, illuminated books, costumes, tiles, book bindings, glass and textiles, lacquered doors, and—the *pièce de résistance*—a remarkable jade jug, all show the atmosphere of refinement and luxury in which those societies lived, with their high level of culture and deep sense of religion. The gallery of the Islamic East is thus one of the most important sections of the museum, and was especially conceived on a spacious scale to suggest the atmosphere of light and air characteristic of the original settings.

Porcelain and stoneware from China as well as lacquerware and prints from Japan are to be found in the gallery devoted to the Far East, which ends the Oriental art section of the museum. This group of objects well illustrates the collector's taste for the exuberant and colorful floral decoration to be found in the various kinds of art he acquired. Here that taste is represented by the famous porcelains of the period from the end of the Ming through the Qing dynasties, with their somewhat Baroque ornamentation and incomparable technical skill.

As the characteristics of the European artworks in the collection demand, the circuit designed for that part of the museum is quite different from that containing art of the East. The intention here was again to create an appropriate atmosphere, one that to some extent corresponds to the original settings of the works of art. The European art section contains a large number of works, including decorative arts from various countries and times, and the visitor thus gets an overall view of the various styles and movements of European art from the eleventh through the mid-twentieth centuries.

This section begins with a series of ivory diptychs and triptychs from France, from the eleventh and fourteenth centuries. Over the years, Gulbenkian acquired an important library, from which are displayed in the museum various examples not only of illuminated manuscripts but also of printed books from France from the sixteenth to the twentieth century. Several illuminated manuscripts on parchment, mostly originating from famous collections and attributed to well-known artists, represent the art of the book in the museum.

The Gulbenkian Museum's important collection of European paintings is exhibited together with sculpture and decorative arts in a chronological sequence from the fifteenth to the twentieth century. Although some of the great art movements are not present in the collection, others, such as the German, Flemish, French, Dutch, English, and Italian schools are represented, in many cases by masterpieces. Fifteenth-century painting in the museum includes works by Stephan Lochner, Dirc Bouts, and Roger van der Weyden. The seventeenth-century Flemish and Dutch school includes paintings by the great artists Rembrandt and Rubens, and the Gulbenkian Collection owns some of their most important masterworks. The museum's Italian collection begins with the fifteenth century and continues through the eighteenth, which is represented by a series of Guardi canvases of exceptional quality, in which Venice is the central theme. Major portraits by Gainsborough, Romney, Hoppner, and Lawrence represent English painting of the late eighteenth century and early nineteenth, together with excellent landscapes by Turner. French painting completes this section, with numerous representative works from the eighteenth and nineteenth centuries. The *fête galante* landscape and mythological scene are favorite themes of Fragonard, Robert, and Boucher and were admired by Gulbenkian as well; the great portrait painters, such as Watteau, Largillière, Nattier, Lepicié and La Tour, also appealed strongly to the collector and their works are prominent in these galleries. The repertoire of French painting of the nineteenth century in the museum is vast, ranging from artists of the Barbizon and Honfleur schools—among them Corot, Millet, Lepine, and Fantin Latour—to Manet, Degas, and Renoir, and culminating in the master of the Impressionist movement, Monet.

The sculpture collection, which is especially strong in works of the French school of the eighteenth and nineteenth centuries, is distributed among the various galleries of European art, with works from the Middle Ages to the twentieth century. Pieces by Coysevox, Tylmen Riemanschneider, and Giambologna, among others, represent the fourteenth through the seventeenth century. Among the sculptures of the following century, particularly notable are works by Pigalle and Falconet, Caffieri and Lemoyne, Clodion and Houdon, with the latter's statue of the huntress Diana standing as the masterpiece of that remarkable artist. Barye, Dalou, and Carpeaux illustrate sculpture of the nineteenth century. However, the art of Auguste Rodin dominates the end of this period, and the Gulbenkian Collection includes several of his works, an especially important piece being the figure of Jean d'Aire, from the group *The Burghers of Calais*.

European art of the Renaissance and Baroque is also represented by sixteenth-century tapestries from the most important production centers of the time, Flanders and Italy. The section is rounded out by a small number of maiolica pieces, fine velvets from the fifteenth, sixteenth, and seventeenth centuries, and a series of medallions from Renaissance Italy, fine and rare examples of the form.

In the field of eighteenth-century art, pride of place goes to France, not only in painting, but also in other media. The refined perfection of technique, and the beauty and formal elegance of French decorative arts particularly interested Gulbenkian, who gathered important groups and pieces for his collection. He was especially attracted to fine French furniture of the *Empire*, Louis XV, and Louis XVI periods, and rare silver by notable French craftsmen of the eighteenth and nineteenth centuries. His collection also includes objects of the highest documentary, artistic, and historical value: tapestries, textiles, bronze objects, porcelain, and other objects of various kinds. The museum has works by such artists as Cressent, Riesener, Jacob, Durand, Germain, Roettier, and others. Gulbenkian was a patron and friend of the artist René Lalique and amassed a major collection of works by him which, in accordance with the founder's ideas, is housed in a room especially designed in the art nouveau style. It contains 169 wrought-metal, jewelled, and colored-glass objects. This fine collection, unique in the world, has found its proper setting at the end of the circuit of galleries.

Apart from the permanent exhibition galleries, the museum building also has its own installations for the Technical and Administrative Services, a temporary exhibition room, an art library, Documentation Center, reserves, strong room, refrigeration and disinfection area, book restoration workshop, and a snack bar for the public.

The Calouste Gulbenkian Museum brings together an art collection of exceptional value and diversity, housed according to up-to-date museological standards, and is today a national and international meeting place at the service of culture.

Maria Teresa Gomes Ferreira,
Director

Introduction

Surrounded by beautifully landscaped gardens, the Calouste Gulbenkian Foundation and its museum are a peaceful oasis amidst the noise and bustle of the city of Lisbon. The foundation, established shortly after Gulbenkian's death in 1955, is devoted to welfare, art, education, and science, and is the largest private charitable institution outside of the United States. The museum, which opened in 1969, both supplements the work and research of the foundation, and stands alone as a unique and extraordinary collection of art. Indeed, it houses one of the most ambitious art collections ever assembled by one man.

To appreciate the collection, it is necessary to understand the man who created it—not an easy task, for Calouste Gulbenkian, while the object of public curiosity during his lifetime, remained secretive and guarded in his private life. Although after several biographies more is known about him today, his life and personality still retain an aura of mystery.

He came from an Armenian family of provincial bankers who had established themselves in Istanbul, then the capital of the Ottoman Empire. His father, Sarkis Gulbenkian, founded his fortune in trading carpets. He later expanded his business by investing in petroleum as well as banking. A story has it that when Calouste was a child, his father rewarded his work at school by giving him fifty piasters. The boy, who liked to visit the bazaars that filled the city, ran off to a coin dealer. After much bargaining, he managed to buy several antique coins. Although his father reproached him for having "squandered" his meager savings, the coins were both remarkable and valuable. This was the first instance of his rare instinct for beauty and quality—the foundation of the fabulous collection to come.

As a young man he achieved considerable expertise in judging Oriental carpets. In 1891, at the age of twenty-two, he published a book entitled *La Transcaucasie et la Peninsula d'Apcheron—Souvenirs de voyage*. This journal contained a chapter on the history, workmanship, materials, dyes, and designs of Oriental carpets and discussed the importance they had in the economic life of Persia. This book revealed his combined interests: art and business.

Calouste Gulbenkian soon went into business on his own. He had inherited his father's business acumen, and by the time he was in his forties, had become a multimillionaire. This was due to one of the most brilliant investments of this century. Shortly before the outbreak of World War I, Gulbenkian, recognizing the potential of oil and petroleum,

The Calouste Gulbenkian Museum in Lisbon

negotiated a five-percent share of the new oil fields that had just been discovered in Iraq. In 1920 this deal was confirmed by the San Remo Oil Company and Gulbenkian was assured of an annual income of several million dollars. This deal was unique in that it granted rights to an individual investor that had up to then been reserved only for sovereign states. He was thereafter known as "Mr. Five-Percent," and became a legend in the world of commerce, from the Arabian oil fields to the offices of Wall Street.

This daring and insightful talent for negotiation was also key to the art collection that he began to assemble. He had wide interests in both Western and Eastern art, and though his earliest acquisitions were not particularly noteworthy, he started, little by little, to amass exceptional pieces.

As Gulbenkian became more seriously involved in acquiring works of art he started to set down certain goals. Whenever he travelled, he made copious notes on the works

The dining room in the Paris house

he saw in various museums. This was not done with the aim of improving his knowledge of art so much as to keep track of the works he wished to purchase should they ever come on the art market. No one took greater pleasure than he in negotiating a deal, enjoying the battle of wits required for a successful outcome. The purchases he made from the Soviet government between 1928 and 1930 were perhaps his greatest coup as a collector. At the time, the Soviets, under Stalin's five-year plan, were in need of foreign currency and were tentatively willing to sacrifice their national art treasures. Naturally, they did not want to make the sale of works from the Hermitage public, and Gulbenkian understood the

delicacy of their position. Even at the first stages of the deal the international press was reporting rumors of such a sale, and questions were raised over the government's right to dispose of the prized works of art. Gulbenkian's rivals, like the well-known international dealer Joseph Duveen, were prepared to pay much higher prices for the Hermitage pieces, but their aggressive tactics and lack of discretion displeased the Soviets. Gulbenkian, on the other hand, was both politic and diplomatic, recognizing the government's need to save face. In a letter of July 17, 1930 to Georges Piatakoff, governor of the State Bank in Moscow, he wrote: "You know that I have always held the opinion that the objects which have been in your museums for many years should not be sold. Not only do they represent a national heritage, but they are also a great source of culture and a source of pride for the nation. . . . Sell anything you want which is not out of museums, but to touch the national patrimony will only arouse serious suspicions. . . . You will ask me why I write this when I myself am persevering in the negotiations for purchasing these pieces. You will probably remember what I have always said and what I continue to say to your representatives; do not sell the objects in your museums, but if you do sell, then I would like to have first refusal at the same price you would offer them to others and I have asked to be kept informed about which works of art you wish to sell."

Several contracts were drawn up with the *Antikvariat*. The first one covered the negotiation for twenty-four French silver and gold objects; two paintings by Hubert Robert, depicting the construction of the gardens at Versailles (pages 94–95); a painting by Dirc Bouts, *The Annunciation* (page 49); and a Louis XVI writing desk by Riesener, decorated with marquetry and gilt bronze (page 87). The total price for these works was £54,000. The second contract was for a group of fifteen silver objects, several paintings, and the great portrait of Hélène Fourment by Rubens (page 75); for these Gulbenkian paid only £155,000. The nervousness of the Soviets had led them to reject his original offer of £150,000 for the silver alone; he then reduced his bid, saying he would only increase it if he could purchase a Rubens and a Giorgione as well. After long negotiations, Gulbenkian purchased both the silver and the Rubens for only £5,000 over his first bid. This deal was perhaps his most masterful, and it took over four months to complete. In this fashion, Gulbenkian was able to appropriate some of the finest works for sale at the time.

There are many anecdotes about Gulbenkian and his various dealings, but the most revealing is the one concerning the flamboyant dealer Duveen. Not only did Gulbenkian outwit him during the Hermitage contracts, but further encounters proved Gulbenkian not only the more astute businessman, but also the finer connoisseur. In a biography of Duveen, S.N. Behrman recounted that Duveen never made as much money out of Gulbenkian as he did from his American clients. When he visited Gulbenkian in Lisbon, he was informed that the owner of three English paintings—a Reynolds, a Lawrence, and a Gainsborough—wished to sell them, but only on the condition that all three be purchased for an inclusive price. Gulbenkian said that he wanted only one of the three, but refused to reveal which. However, he offered to tell Duveen the name of the owner in exchange

Two sphinxes: Calouste Gulbenkian on a visit to Egypt

for first choice from among the group should Duveen buy the paintings. He made the further condition that before he told Duveen which one he wanted, the dealer was to price them individually, with a sum total not exceeding the purchase price paid for the three. Duveen accepted the proposal and bought the paintings. He then tried to outguess his client. He decided that Gulbenkian, being an Oriental, would choose the most showy and opulent of the three, the Lawrence, which he accordingly priced disproportionately high. Conversely, by the terms of the proposal, the other two were quite inexpensive. But Gulbenkian was a true connoisseur: he purchased the loveliest of the three, the Gainsborough portrait of Mrs. Lowndes-Stone (page 89). As

The courtyard of the Gulbenkian residence in Paris

Behrman pointed out, "It was one of the few times anyone acquired a Duveen without paying a Duveen price for it."

It was by such maneuvers as this that Gulbenkian managed to build a matchless collection. His tastes were catholic, and his collection was one of the few truly to encompass the art of both East and West. Gulbenkian once wrote, "My aim is to make a very fine collection . . . from an artistic point of view. In this respect I want to confine myself to such specimens as are of the finest preservation and the most remarkable beauty. I do not want rarities if they do not at the same time respond to the above characteristics." Indeed, Gulbenkian insisted on the perfect condition of all his acquisitions. To George Davey of Knoedler and Company he wrote, "By temperament I am not a specific collector of periods or series, but just as with my pictures, I like to possess the finest specimens—You know my collection. I have not many pieces, but I want them to be of the highest quality."

Like many collectors, Gulbenkian also put a high value on the provenance of his pieces. While he was proud of their quality and authenticity, he took special pleasure in the knowledge that he owned works of art that had previ-

ously belonged to notable historic figures. This was particularly true of his collection of French decorative art. For example, he acquired a desk that once belonged to Marie Antoinette and a pair of silver mustard pots (page 93) that had once adorned the tables of Mme de Pompadour.

Gulbenkian was a true epicure in many respects. At the same time he was an intensely private person. He was reluctant to open his collection to the public, so instead of inviting strangers to his house, he loaned various pieces to public museums. In 1934 he lent some of his most outstanding paintings and sculptures to the National Gallery in London. Later, the National Gallery of Art in Washington benefitted from a similar loan. Works from his collection of French paintings and decorative arts were put on display in French museums for some time. Indeed, Gulbenkian did not attempt to assemble his collection in one location until he moved to Paris. He then built a sumptuous mansion on the Avenue d'Iéna that housed much of his collection. Here he became a recluse, surrounded by his works of art, which he named "my children." When asked why he chose to remain in such seclusion, hiding his treasures from most eyes, Gulbenkian would reply that he was an Oriental, and that the Orientals were not in the habit of unveiling the women of their harems.

Gulbenkian also loved nature. Before the outbreak of World War I he bought land near Deauville in Normandy, about eighty-four acres in all. Here he designed elaborate gardens but built no mansion. Les Enclos, as he called it, was a beautiful estate with terraces, tree-lined avenues, fountains, and hidden retreats. Whenever he could, he spent a few weeks in summer there. He wrote to his landscape architect, M. Duchêne, "It must not be forgotten that what I want above all is that the park should have a romantic character." Later he wrote, "My great desire is to achieve a harmonious whole. . . . I want to keep the romantic character of the property, to emphasize it and to beautify it, not to stylize it." Gulbenkian's romanticism also prompted him to cultivate orchids and to breed birds, and he kept many rare and exotic species at the house in Paris. In 1940, a few days before the German occupation of the city, he left for Vichy. His office heard nothing from him for two weeks and the staff waited anxiously for news. When a telegram finally did arrive, it was frantically opened. It read, "Don't forget to feed the birds!"

Gulbenkian spent the final years of his life in Portugal. He lived at the Hotel Aviz in Lisbon, often driving out to visit the beautiful towns of Cascais, Estoril, and Sintra. He no longer had to see "his children," which remained in Paris. It was during these years that he decided that his

The grand salon *of Calouste Gulbenkian's Paris home*

collection should be housed in a single museum after his death. At one time the National Gallery in London hoped to inherit the collection, as did the National Gallery of Art in Washington. However, Gulbenkian decided against such donations, preferring to maintain his collection not only intact but as an autonomous whole which would reflect his taste and preserve his memory. After his death, Dr. José Perdigão, his attorney, succeeded in gathering all the dispersed masterpieces in Lisbon, despite French efforts to keep the works that had been loaned to their national museums. Until the museum could be built, these pieces were on display at the Palacio Pombal at Oeiras. Today his foundation, built on the fortune he created, enjoys an independent life of its own. The collection is housed in a modern building in the midst of a public park. The museum functions as a cultural center; the structure includes not only galleries but a concert and lecture hall, and an administration building which acts as the focus of the foundation's multinational operations.

The number, range, and quality of works in the Gulbenkian Museum never ceases to astound. It is unique in its scope and value, especially when one considers that it was all brought together in this century by a single man. Ironically, although Calouste Gulbenkian remained an enigma during his life, and closed his collection to all but a lucky few, by building such a foundation, he ensured that he would be remembered and that "his children" would be a monument to his flamboyant genius.

Plate List

*The
Egyptian
Collection*

EGYPTIAN

Ka Figure of a Man

Middle Kingdom, eleventh or twelfth
  dynasty
Polychromed wood
69 cm. high (27 3/8 in.)
Inventory no. 142

This wooden funerary statue of a *ka* figure represents a vigorous man striding forward, with the right hand at his side and the left raised before him. Originally, his clenched fists held a staff and a scepter, representing the deceased man's authority. The original rectangular base and the man's feet have been lost. Naturalistic polychromy enhances the lifelike quality of this powerful figure: the flesh is painted a shade of red typically used in Egyptian art for males; the round, curly wig is black, and black too are the brows, while the eyes were originally inlaid. The type of wig is unusual in two ways: it stops short of the ear lobes, which are more commonly covered by such wigs, and the curls are represented by circles stamped into the surface. The man's kilt is actually canvas, coated with fine plaster and painted white. Broad-shouldered and muscular, the figure suggests exceptional physical prowess, while the square, smiling face expresses confidence and determination. All of these characteristics endow him with powerful vitality: although representing a dead man, the statue appears alive. That this was the intention of the Egyptian craftsman and his patron is demonstrated by the purpose of such figures, which was to house the *ka*, or soul, of the deceased. In this sense, then, the figure was indeed alive, and capable of accepting offerings presented to it. According to Egyptian belief, an individual's immortality was assured if his *ka* were provided with a body, such as this figure, while his spirit, the *ba*, travelled to its final resting place.

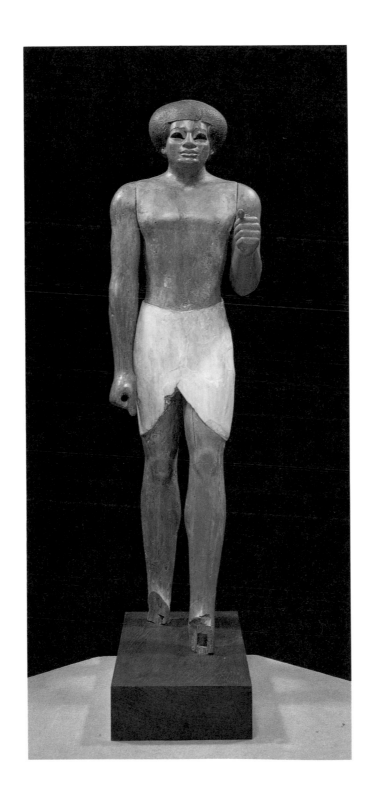

EGYPTIAN

Head of Amenemhāt III (?)

Middle Kingdom, twelfth dynasty
Obsidian
12 cm. high (4 3/4 in.)
Inventory no. 138

The head of Amenemhāt III (the "MacGregor Head," so called after its previous owner), part of a statuette of the pharaoh, is carved of black obsidian, or natural glass, an extremely hard mineral. The Egyptian predilection for such hard materials is related to the belief that in order to achieve immortality the soul must remain in a body. Physical damage to the body or to representations of the body was tantamount to crippling the eternal home of the spirit. Hard substances, then, were preferred because they were durable and hence could be used with comparative safety for physical representations, which were required to preserve the soul should its mortal body become corrupt. This belief in eternal life is the self-confident core of the Egyptian ethos, which is of necessity closely tied to its art. The credo of certain immortality is expressed in the perfect symmetry and cubic form of the "MacGregor Head," achieved by carving the obsidian inward from the four sides of the original block. The eternal regularity of the ideal is important, rather than the vagaries and ephemera of temporal life.

So vivid is the depiction of the pharaoh's face that a modern spectator may be tempted to view it as a portrait likeness. In fact, it is not a portrait in the modern sense, but a generalized visual ideal of kingship. However, while the Old Kingdom dynasties emphasized the king's divinity, perfection, and infallibility, the Middle Kingdom pharaoh was interpreted as the just protector of his people, alone with his great burden of leadership. Austerity has replaced the graceful self-assurance of the Old Kingdom apparent in the first plate of the book. The Middle Kingdom ruler is the good shepherd of his nation who must always be wakeful and watchful, always concerned with justice for gods and for men. The formal throne name of Amenemhāt III reflects this concern: he is called "Justice belongs to the God Re." The lines of the monarch's face are the idealized visible testimony of his kingly duty.

21

EGYPTIAN

Funerary Figure of a Man

New Kingdom, eighteenth dynasty
Polychromed wood
25 cm. high (9 7/8 in.)
Inventory no. 121A

The purpose and stance of this figure are almost identical to the Middle Kingdom *ka* figure illustrated on page 19. Carved of wood, the statue is painted in naturalistic colors, red for the body, black for wig and brows, and white for the loincloth. The stance, a step forward with both feet flat on the ground and the legs straight, is derived from the hieroglyph for walking. The hands originally held the deceased's attributes: a scepter and a staff. Such sculptures housed the soul or *ka* of an individual after his death, and the unchanging Egyptian belief in immortality was asserted in their art by a vocabulary of types, forms, and poses that remained essentially unchanged for many centuries. Nonetheless, there is remarkable stylistic diversity within the strict, self-imposed limitations of Egyptian art. This New Kingdom figure illustrates various stylistic developments and decorative refinements. The proportions are much more slender than those of the Old and Middle Kingdoms. Without seeming to be fragile—which would be inappropriate to a figure meant to embody the soul—the New Kingdom statue is slim and elegant. His left elbow projects into space, so that his silhouette departs from the strict adherence to the block-shape of the older styles. The wig is carved in successive layers of vertical ridges. Folds in the kilt are varied: the fabric is pulled across the hips and knotted at the waist, and diagonal pleats are juxtaposed with curving lines. Such decorative details ornament the figure, endowing it with the cosmopolitan elegance characteristic of the New Kingdom.

23

EGYPTIAN

Funerary Figure of Lady Henut-tauy

New Kingdom, eighteenth dynasty
Polychromed wood and gold leaf
29.2 cm. high (11 ½ in.)
Inventory no. 129

The wooden figure of Lady Henut-tauy represents a popular type in New Kingdom art: the figure of the deceased is represented upright, walking forward, standing on a block inscribed with her name and a prayer. The lady's continued existence in the afterlife is assured by the survival of her name in the hieroglyphs, and by the sculptural representation of an immortal body which survived her to offer her prayer forever. Such votive figures are represented as though alive, and yet in a static, even rigid way, because any indication of transience would be inappropriate in an image meant to be eternal. The lady's position is typical of these figures. One leg is before the other, as though she had taken a forward step, yet both feet remain flat on the ground and there is no hint of a natural weight-shift in the body. These legs are in fact the hieroglyph for walking, and this standard pose is intended to be read as "walking," not understood as a realistic representation of that act. The figure is symmetrical—again, because any irregularity would be undesirable in the image of immortality. Her skin-tight gown reveals the contours of her breasts and thighs. The smooth, sensuous surface of the body is contrasted with the ridges of the wig and the gold-leaf necklace. The large eyes are painted in a lifelike manner, and the alert, smiling face expresses typical Egyptian self-confidence. Because Lady Henut-tauy lives forever, she requires food, clothing, and other worldly goods in the afterlife. These are guaranteed by the prayer inscribed in hieroglyphs, a veritable catalogue of provisions. The figure is offered to the god "Ptah-Seker-Osiris . . . that he may give . . . bread, beer, oxen, fowl, alabaster, clothing, incense, and unguent, all things good and pure, to the spirit of . . . Henut-tauy."

25

EGYPTIAN

Funerary Stele of the Scribe Ary

New Kingdom, late eighteenth
  dynasty
Painted compact limestone
29 x 21.6 cm. (11 3/8 x 8 1/2 in.)
Inventory no. 160

The Scribe Ary kneels and offers a perpetual prayer to the divine pharaoh Aahmes I (Neb-pehty-Ra) and his queen, in this commemorative relief formerly in the MacGregor collection. The stele has many traces of the colored paints that once decorated the relief and made the figures seem lifelike. The scribe's kilt is white and his flesh is painted with a reddish tone, typically used in Egyptian art for males. Traces of red are also visible in the hieroglyphs, and green in the offerings. The imagery and formulaic poses reveal the New Kingdom dependence upon Old and Middle Kingdom art and ideas. The stele is divided horizontally, with the scribe and his words below, and above, his offerings to the deified pharaoh and queen in their shrine. Ary's ritual gesture is given emphasis by the unnatural elongation of his fingers. His kneeling pose is derived from the hieroglyph for "worship," seen in the inscription at the lower left. He turns toward the hieroglyphic inscription of his prayer, as though the words become visible as he offers them. The incised hieroglyphs praise the pharaoh and queen, patrons of the Necropolis at Thebes. The Egyptians believed that their monarchs were gods and the children of gods, in a literal physiological sense.

The pharaoh and his queen are represented crowned and enthroned, in profile, turned toward the incised hieroglyphs of their names. The queen embraces her lord, forever the supporting, loving consort, as in other representations of royal couples. Already in Old Kingdom imagery the Egyptians had sought to make immortal such warm human relationships by their representation in art. Aahmes holds the *Ankh*, symbol of life, and the ruler's crook. The royal faces, like that of the scribe, are smiling and confident. This is a New Kingdom revival of the characterizations of Old Kingdom imagery (page 17), instead of the more recent Middle Kingdom expressions of sobriety and concern (page 19).

Pharaoh, queen, and scribe all turn their attention toward the inscribed hieroglyphs that dominate the composition. Egyptians believed in the extraordinary power of written names and words. It is these inscriptions that preserve the individual's identity, just as the hieroglyphs of Ary's pious words preserve his prayer for all time.

27

EGYPTIAN

Statuette of the Courtier Bes

Saite period, twenty-sixth dynasty
Compact limestone
32.2 cm. high (12 $^{11}/_{16}$ in.)
Inventory no. 158

The kings of Sais ruled Egypt briefly between two periods of foreign domination, from the withdrawal of the Assyrians in 663 B.C. until the arrival of the Persians in 525. The Courtier Bes lived during the reign of the first Saite king, Psammetichus I (Psamtik). In this period, traditional Egyptian imagery was revived as a reassertion of national identity. Thus the courtier's squatting pose is intentionally archaic, a deliberate reference to Egypt's glorious past, to prouder and more secure times. The sculpture is carved from a block of limestone, the original form of which is preserved in the base and in the plinth in back of the figure. The sculptor has cut inward from the surface, carving each of the four planes separately, so that the finished figure maintains the cubic form of the block. The pose combines an easy, naturalistic representation of a squatting man while yet retaining the rigid geometry of the original stone, which survives in places: between the torso and arms and between the legs, areas which have not been cut out. This insistently geometric treatment endows the figure with a sense of strength and permanence. This was of course the intention of such funerary sculptures, the purpose of which was to visualize Egyptian belief in immortality. Bes's smile may be understood as an expression of confidence in that belief, and as an indication of lifelike vitality in the face. The sculpture is incised with several all-important inscriptions which preserve the courtier's identity and make his prayer eternal. The hieroglyphs address the gods Horus and Isis on behalf of Bes, apologize for his earthly life, and identify him repeatedly by name and rank, indicating the great importance invested by the Egyptians in the written name. The soul may inhabit the mummy and other representations of the deceased only if his identity is explicitly preserved in this way.

29

EGYPTIAN

Relief Study for the Portrait of a Pharaoh

Early Ptolemaic period
Sandstone
21 x 18 cm. (8 1/4 x 7 1/8 in.)
Inventory no. 167

One of the finest—and most famous—examples of Egyptian art in the Gulbenkian Museum is the exquisite early Ptolemaic head of a pharaoh. The pharaoh is seen in profile, according to the formula already established in the Old Kingdom (page 17), with the eye and shoulders seen frontally. He wears an elaborate collar and the pharaonic crown, decorated with two symbolic creatures. At the back, the Hawk God Horus spreads his wings as though to embrace the pharaoh's head, symbolizing the god's protection of the ruler—in fact, the god's identity with the pharaoh. Among the pharaoh's titles was that of "Horus," the sky-god who established the divine lineage of the kings of Egypt as the heirs of his father, the god Osiris. Horus is particularly associated with Upper Egypt.

The crown is also decorated in front, above the pharaoh's brow, with a cobra, twisting as though alive. This refers to Lower Egypt, and again signifies divine protection. The surface of the crown is further embellished with a design of concentric circles. Originally the sculpture was painted, and its color would have enhanced the decorative splendor of the relief.

The surfaces of the face and the forms of the ear are carved with delicate modulations of the stone, suggesting the softness of flesh. These smooth surfaces are juxtaposed with the textured areas of the collar and crown, and with the crystalline precision of line and contour. The decorative exuberance and sophistication of the relief are matched by the mood of the sculpture, the pharaoh's large eye and smiling lips conveying his power, indeed, his divinity as descendant of the gods and unquestioned ruler of Upper and Lower Egypt.

31

EGYPTIAN

Mummy Mask

Thirtieth dynasty
Silver gilt
43.5 cm. high (17 1/8 in.)
Inventory no. 62

All Egyptian funerary art is predicated upon the belief that the immortality of the soul, the *ka*, depends upon the preservation of the name and body of the deceased. The practice of mummification was designed to sustain the earthly body, even after death, for the immortal *ka*. Viscera were removed and kept separately, usually in canopic jars, to be entombed together with the mummy. The corpse was dessicated and shrouded in tight bands of cloth and finally encased in a sarcophagus shaped much like the body itself. The head and face might be covered by a luxurious mask, such as this silver gilt example, fashioned in the *repoussé* technique, that is, hammered on a mold. The ideal, symmetrical features of the elegant face, the smooth, rounded forms of the headdress and, above all, the shining splendor of the gilt silver endow the mask with an otherworldly quality, suggesting the timelessness of eternity. These standardized abstractions are, however, combined with certain lifelike features, namely the brown color of the brows and pupils, the self-possessed smile, and the wide, steady gaze. The face is thus both alive and assured, yet with no indication of the ephemeral nature of earthly life. It is the face of one who has overcome mortality.

The
European
Collection

THE COGHILL PAINTER

Red-Figure Krater

Greek, ca. 450 B.C.
Glazed earthenware
42 cm. high (16 ½ in.)
Inventory no. 682

Although appreciated by the ancients as objects of considerable beauty and refinement, vases were also made to perform certain practical functions. This krater, found at Agrigento, was used by the Greeks for mixing wine and water. The technique of painting is called red figure: figures and decorative details are in fact the unpainted clay of the vase, while the background is glazed black. Thus, forms are defined by their silhouettes, and the modelling of details of faces, musculature, and drapery are drawn with fine black lines. The sophistication of this art is such that the individual styles of numerous Greek vase painters can be recognized. The artist of the Gulbenkian vase is called the Coghill Painter after the former owner of another vase by the same master.

The vase is divided into two horizontal zones by decorative bands of ornament. Each field is populated by lively groups of figures who run around the body of the vase, enacting two separate but related stories. The upper register is devoted to the story of the Rape of the Daughters of Leukippos. The name Leukippos means "white-horse-man," referring to this nobleman's splendid horses. His two daughters had already been betrothed when they were carried off by the twin sons of Zeus, Kastor and Polydeukes. The women's promised husbands attacked, and only Polydeukes survived. Not wishing to live without his brother, he prayed to his divine father to allow him to share his immortality with Kastor. This was granted, and, according to the myth, the twins alternate between life and death. The brothers eventually came to be identified with the constellation Gemini.

Below this heroic and tragic tale is that of another amorous assault. Maenads, women devoted to the cult of the god Dionysos, run frantically, trying to escape a lusty satyr. The satyr's arms and legs are spread wide as though he would grasp two maenads at once, and his tail flies behind him as he dashes frenetically after one of them. This comic episode counterbalances the more sober tale of the Daughters of Leukippos.

37

FRENCH

Illuminated Manuscript Page

Ca. 1300
Parchment
53 x 34.5 cm. (20 7/8 x 13 5/8 in.)
Inventory no. M.1

This illuminated manuscript page from a book of sacred songs gives the music and lyric in commemoration of the Annunciation, to be sung at vespers on the Feast of St. Gregory the Great.

The initial "O" adorns the word *orietur,* "let us rise." Both the illumination and the paleography are in the style of the Cholet group of manuscripts, which were commissioned by Jean, Cardinal Cholet, in the late thirteenth century, and which include volumes in the Biblioteca Nazionale, Florence, and the Bibliothèque Nationale in Paris. The vertical bar of the letter is decorated with a geometric pattern and inhabited by two figures, one bearded and with the legs of an animal, the other an almost nude youth. The tails of the letter flow into the upper and lower margins, swirling into tendrils ornamented with small globes and with stylized leaves. A strange creature with a human head perches on the lower branch. The central section is a circle within a rectangular frame, the background painted with a diaper pattern of squares. A trefoil Gothic arch with delicate crockets serves both to enframe the figures and to suggest an architectural setting for the narrative. The central scene is the Annunciation, the announcement by the Archangel Gabriel to the Virgin Mary that she is to bear the Christ Child. The figures are graceful and slender, and Mary especially seems to sway against the background. Their garments are carefully modelled in light and shade, forming varied abstract patterns. The faces are drawn with delicate lines on the pale flesh. The moment represented and the words of Gabriel's salutation refer to the adjacent text. His wings folded behind him, the Angel steps toward the Madonna as he addresses her with the words inscribed on his scroll, *Ave Gracia plena,* "Hail, full of grace." Mary's gesture indicates acknowledgement of Gabriel's words, and the tilt of her head implies acceptance of her sacred role.

FRENCH

Diptych: Scenes from the Passion

Early fourteenth century
Ivory
19.5 x 23 cm. (7 ^{11}/16 in. x 9 ^{1}/16 in.)
Inventory no. 125

Ivory carvings such as this diptych were made as images for private devotion. The two leaves of the diptych are separate and attached by hinges, so that the piece may be closed and easily carried. Each leaf is framed by a simple molding and divided horizontally by a row of evenly spaced flowers. This is the so-called rose decoration, used in the first half of the fourteenth century to separate different narrative episodes, instead of the architectural framing preferred in earlier ivories. Each section contains one or more scenes. In style and composition, these episodes of the Passion are related to contemporary manuscript painting. Indeed, ivories were originally decorated with color and gilding and closely resembled manuscript painting. Traces of color survive in this piece, in the garments of some of the figures.

The diptych presents the most painful scenes of the Passion, focusing exclusively on Christ's suffering and death. The cycle begins at the lower left with the Flagellation and Christ bearing the Cross. Above this is the Crucifixion. Christ's head falls limply on his chest; his arms are distended by the weight of his body, which falls in a pathetic zigzag on the cross. He is flanked by mourners, including the Virgin, who swoons, pressing her hand to her breast as she views her son. The cycle continues with the scene at the upper right, the Deposition, in which Christ's body is taken down from the Cross, while he is mourned on earth by his associates and in the heavens by angels. Below, the narrative concludes with the Entombment, in which Christ's body is laid to rest in a coffin. In each of these scenes the narrative is told almost exclusively by figures alone: no environment is created for them and only the most essential props are included. Tall and slender, the figures sway gracefully against a flat ground, and all are aligned on one frontal plane in the shallow depth created for them. Faces are rarely expressive, and emotion is conveyed largely by posture and gesture. Christ is central in each scene, enframed by the other characters, who generally turn and gesture toward Him. The attention of the viewer and worshipper is likewise focused upon Christ.

41

STEFAN LOCHNER

b. Meersburg am Bodensee, ca. 1420
d. Cologne, 1451

The Presentation in the Temple

Dated: *1445*
Tempera and oil (?) on panel
33.5 x 22.5 cm. (13 3/16 in. x
   8 7/8 in.)
Inventory no. 272

Lochner's *Presentation in the Temple*, dated 1445 at the top of the fictive stone arch, is a section from an altarpiece dedicated to the Virgin. The master has represented the *Presentation in the Temple* with great tenderness and intimacy of feeling. He establishes this mood in several ways. Most important are the actions of the Child and the High Priest Simeon: the priest embraces the Infant, who raises his hand to caress the old man's face, and the two exchange an intense glance, which binds them together emotionally as well as physically. Meanwhile, the Madonna and the prophet Anna act as pious witnesses, and St. Joseph waits with two doves, his offering to the Temple. The figures are pressed close together around the altar, and the surrounding arch limits the space, further enhancing the feeling of intimacy. The arch functions both as the frontal terminus of the architecture and as an illusionistic frame for the scene.

Lochner has delighted in representing the effects of light on different surfaces and textures. Coming from the left, the light shines through the transparent altar canopy, casting a delicate shadow on the stone wall, and glistening on the precious jewels of the priest's sumptuous gown. Such exquisite effects make the painting itself seem like a precious object. In this respect, Lochner's style was strongly influenced by the art of Jan van Eyck.

A secondary light source shines through the stained-glass window where Moses is represented with the Tablets of the Law. The significance is clear: Christ's presentation, that is, his formal dedication to God, refers to the establishment of the New Covenant, understood as superseding the Old Law of Moses.

43

ROGER VAN DER WEYDEN

b. Brussels, 1399/1400
d. Brussels, 1464

St. Joseph

Ca. 1460
Tempera and oil(?) on panel
20.7 x 18.2 cm. (8 1/8 x 7 3/16 in.)
Inventory no. 79.B

Roger van der Weyden is one of the greatest and most influential masters of fifteenth-century Netherlandish painting, and this fragment from an altarpiece is a superb example of his art. Together with Roger's *St. Catherine*, discussed on the following page, *St. Joseph* formed part of a large altarpiece of which another section is preserved in the National Gallery, London, showing *St. Mary Magdalen Reading*. The London fragment of Roger's altarpiece includes the body of old St. Joseph, holding crystal prayer beads and leaning on his walking stick. Roger's characterization of St. Joseph is poignant. He shows the upper part of the figure with bent shoulders and the head forward, moving toward the image of the Madonna (now lost), originally the central figure of the complete altarpiece. Joseph stands next to an open window, through which is visible a distant landscape and cloudy blue sky. The saint's bent posture suggests at once his advanced age and his pious devotion: his physical weakness enriches the expression of his spiritual strength. Of course, it is above all the saint's face that communicates his character and his piety. Roger convinces the spectator of the tangible reality of his interpretation: we feel that we behold a portrait likeness of St. Joseph, a representation that makes him seem truly alive before us. The master's depiction is persuasive visually and compelling psychologically. Roger's acute observations of details of the face—the network of wrinkles, the stubble of beard, the teary moisture of the eyes, the slight parting of the lips—all these make the figure real. Concurrently, these precise physical aspects express the spiritual life of the saint, his asceticism, his great suffering, his deep faith. The psychological reality of Roger's *St. Joseph* guides the viewer's own emotional and spiritual involvement.

45

ROGER VAN DER WEYDEN

St. Catherine

Ca. 1460
Tempera and oil(?) on panel
21.2/21.7 x 18.5 cm.
 (8 9/16 x 7 1/4 in.)
Inventory no. 79A

The exquisite head of St. Catherine is a fragment from the same altarpiece as Roger's *St. Joseph*, on the previous page. The angle of the wall behind St. Catherine and her posture indicate that her original position was to the left of the Madonna and Child in the complete altarpiece. Moreover, the saint's relationship to the window implies that she was shown kneeling. The vista seen through the window includes a graceful swan floating on water that reflects in broken patches the buildings on the shore.

No specific attribute identifies the saint as Catherine, but this seems likely for two reasons. St. Catherine is typically represented as a beautiful young woman, and, being of noble birth, she is richly gowned. Here Roger has clothed the saint splendidly, her fine fabrics embroidered with gold thread, with pearls, and with gemstones. The light entering through the window at the left falls on these various gleaming surfaces, the shimmering gold, glowing pearls, and translucent cabochon gems. Even St. Catherine's hair glistens in the light. In contrast to all these light-reflecting objects, Roger has set a delicate white veil at St. Catherine's neck. The sheer fabric is transparent, so that her flesh is visible through it, but where it is folded, the veil forms white highlights. In addition to these various embellishments, Roger endows the saint with the abstract beauty of geometric forms, stressing the pure oval of her head and the cylinder of her neck. He also gives careful attention to the details of her face and skin, recording fine lines in the neck and around the eyes, which help establish the image as a convincing characterization of an individual.

47

DIRC BOUTS

b. Haarlem, ca. 1420
d. Louvain, 1475

The Annunciation

Ca. 1462–70
Tempera and oil(?) on panel,
  transferred to canvas
27.3 x 34.4 cm. (10 3/4 x 13 9/16 in.)
Inventory no. 628

By representing *The Annunciation* in the Virgin's house, Bouts made that miraculous event more psychologically accessible, more immediate to the contemporary viewer. The house and its furnishings were readily recognizable as a fifteenth-century Netherlandish residence, an historical anachronism that encouraged the worshipper to contemplate the miracle with a sense of its personal and eternal relevance. This is not the Annunciation interpreted as one particular historical event, fixed in place and time. It is the story of the Annunciation narrated in and for Bouts's own time and for all time, signifying the pertinence of the miracle to men in their everyday lives.

The Archangel Gabriel has just entered Mary's room and begins to genuflect—his knees are bent but do not yet touch the pavement. The Archangel looks at the Virgin and raises his hand in greeting, beginning the salutation, "Ave, Maria." The Madonna is kneeling at a prie-dieu where she has been reading the Bible, according to apocryphal accounts of the Annunciation. She turns toward the Archangel with her eyes modestly downcast and presses her left hand to her breast in a gesture suggesting both surprise and acceptance, expressed by her words "Ecce ancilla Dei" ("Behold the handmaiden of the Lord").

The Annunciation is of course also the moment of the Incarnation, and the Holy Spirit, surrounded by brilliant rays of divine light, flies toward Mary, symbolically illuminating her. Her chamber is further flooded by natural sunlight, coming from the left. Bouts explores the various effects of the light on different textures and suggests a space permeated with light and air. Through the door is the brick wall of a closed garden, symbolizing Mary's virginity. And through the window Bouts shows a far landscape vista, with distant mountains blurring in a bluish haze on the horizon. The blues and greens in the background contrast with the warm tones, different shades of red and brown that predominate in the foreground, and the minute forms of the landscape are juxtaposed with the large forms of the figures and Mary's house. A whole world is here created, and with it, intimations of divinity.

PISANELLO

b. Pisa, ca. 1395
d. Rome, 1455

Medal of Niccolò Piccinino

Ca. 1441
Bronze
8.8 cm. in diameter (3 7/16 in.)
Inventory no. 2404

Ancient coins were the obvious model for Renaissance medals, decorated with a profile portrait in bust length on the obverse, and on the reverse, an emblem or symbol. Pisanello is the most famous and the greatest of the medallists of the Italian Renaissance, and the Gulbenkian piece is a splendid example of his medal portraiture. The bust of a man in armor and wearing a tall hat is encircled by an explanatory inscription in Latin: *NICOLAVS. PICININVS. VICECOMES. MARCHIO. CAPITANEVS. MAX. AC. MARS. ALTER.* Pisanello's powerful modelling, simple design, and perceptive treatment of the face convey the energy, sobriety, and forcefulness of the *condottiere* Niccolò Piccinino (1380–1444). Niccolò truly seems to be "*alter mars,*" another Mars, as the inscription claims. The inscription also identifies Piccinino as "*vicecomes,*" suggesting a date around 1441, which would also be consistent with Pisanello's style at that time. In 1441, Piccinino became *vicecomes* and married the daughter of the Duke of Milan, in whose service the *condottiere* fought against the Venetians.

The medal's reverse shows a griffin symbolizing Perugia nursing two infant boys and wearing a collar inscribed *PERVSIA*. This refers to Piccinino's native city, represented by the griffin which supposedly had suckled the sons of Mars. But these children are identified in the inscription as Braccio da Montone and Niccolò Piccinino—literally the sons of Mars to whom Niccolò is likened on the obverse. The inscription on the reverse ends with the artist's signature, signifying the author's pride in his work and the owner's in possessing a medal by Pisanello.

50

obverse

reverse

51

ATTRIBUTED TO ANTONIO ROSSELLINO

b. Settignano, 1427
d. Florence, 1479

Virgin and Child

Undated
Marble relief
94 x 62 cm. (37 x 24 3/8 in.)
Inventory no. 539

Antonio Rossellino certainly designed this relief of the *Virgin and Child*, although another sculptor of the Rossellino shop probably assisted in the actual carving. In style, composition, and characterization, the sculpture resembles another relief by Antonio, in the Metropolitan Museum in New York.

The Madonna is seated in the center of the relief, turned sideways to the right, with the Child in her lap. The arm of her chair, decorated with a bull's head and garlands, appears in the lower left corner. While Mary looks down at her Child, He gazes at an unseen worshipper and gives his blessing. The figures are calm and restrained, physically inactive, but animated by their psychological characterizations. Gentle smiles enliven their faces and suggest beneficence toward the worshipper. Their benign and even friendly mood reflects the self-confidence of Renaissance man. *The Virgin and Child* is typical of Antonio's refined, even delicate taste. Mary is an elegant beauty with fine features and long, tapering fingers. The Infant Christ is a pretty child with curling locks of hair and soft, babylike flesh. Rossellino has endowed the inherently static composition of two seated figures with liveliness and interest. He achieves this in several ways—by the smiles, by Mary's expressive hands, by the play of the folds of drapery, and by variations in the height of the relief. Mary and Christ are carved in the highest relief and therefore seem closest to us, literally in our space. The background is sculpted in lower relief, with *putti* flying in the clouds, hovering around the Madonna and Child. The little angels turn in different directions, but all direct their glance toward the Child, thus also guiding the viewer's attention to Him.

53

LUCA DELLA ROBBIA

b. Florence, 1400
d. Florence, 1482

Faith

Undated
Glazed terra cotta
180 cm. in diameter (70 7/8 in.)
Inventory no. 540

The Florentine Luca della Robbia seems to have perfected the medium of glazed terracotta sculpture for which he was greatly admired by his contemporaries. The roundel or tondo depicting the Theological Virtue *Faith* has been ascribed to Luca or perhaps to his nephew, Andrea della Robbia. The bright yellow, purple, and green of the border and the characteristic Della Robbia combination of a pure white figure with an intense blue ground gave coloristic richness and gleaming brightness to the architectural setting for which the sculpture would have been made. Such circular reliefs were used as ceiling decorations, for example, Luca's ceiling in the Chapel of the Cardinal of Portugal in the church of San Miniato in Florence. For such use the lightness of terra cotta (compared to stone reliefs) was an advantage. It has been suggested that the relief of *Faith* might have been made for the Pazzi Chapel at Santa Croce in Florence. In any case, this tondo was certainly one of a group representing the Virtues, and perhaps including also the reliefs depicting the Cardinal Virtues of *Temperance* (now in the Cluny Museum in Paris) and *Prudence* (at the Metropolitan Museum in New York). However, *Temperance* and *Prudence* lack the inner cord-molding used in the *Faith* relief, which suggests that they may have been modelled for a different cycle of the Virtues.

It was customary to personify the Virtues as women, and *Faith* is indeed a beautiful woman, calm and serious, holding her traditional attributes, the Cross and the chalice of the Mass. Although she stands upright, she turns her head and her glance to the right. Possibly *Faith* once turned in order to face the altar of the chapel for which the relief was made. Or perhaps she turned to look toward a central medallion of the Holy Dove, when the tondo was in its original ceiling location. Luca had used a central tondo of the Dove in the Portuguese Chapel in San Miniato.

The background of the *Faith* relief is Della Robbia's characteristic blue, with indications of clouds below, to suggest the sky. Thus the figure seems to disappear in the clouds, as though she were appearing in the heavens. The frame enhances this illusion. Within a classical egg-and-dart motif, Della Robbia has sculpted a wreath of leaves and fruits, citrons and grapes. A simple white molding completes the frame, which may be understood as a round window open to the sky to reveal the figure. The contrast of the pure white of *Faith* with the rich colors of the background and frame heightens the impression of the Virtue as an otherworldly apparition.

55

DOMENICO GHIRLANDAIO

b. Florence, 1449
d. Florence, 1494

Portrait of a Young Woman

Ca. 1480–90
Tempera on panel
44 x 32 cm. (17 5/16 x 12 5/8 in.)
Inventory no. 282

Earlier in the fifteenth century, Italian portraitists had represented figures in profile (as in Pisanello's medal, page 51). But after about 1475, artists began to show frontal views of faces, while yet retaining the traditional bust-length format of the older profile portraits. Domenico Ghirlandaio was among the most successful painters in late fifteenth-century Florence, and his workshop (which included the young Michelangelo) was among the most active. The unidentified *Young Woman* in this panel, dating from around 1490, reveals the qualities that made Ghirlandaio's art so popular with his contemporaries. The young woman has an immediate, almost tangible presence. In part, Ghirlandaio achieves this by placing the lady in the foreground, close to the viewer, so that her arms and shoulders are partially truncated by the edges of the panel. By painting the background black, Ghirlandaio focuses all attention on the young woman: no distracting references to her environment are included, no other forms or colors rival her. Ghirlandaio's figure, unlike many other late fifteenth-century Italian portraits, does not look at the viewer, but rather toward her companion, perhaps her sister, in the pendant to this portrait (now in the National Gallery, London). Both ladies have similar coiffures and both wear bead necklaces and sheer bodices clasped by a single button. Ghirlandaio's attention to such details of fashion was an important aspect of his portraits, both visually and as an indication of the sitter's status. The master's depiction of the *Young Woman* convinces the spectator of his objectivity; one believes that Ghirlandaio recorded accurately what he saw, and this straightforward quality of the portrait in turn implies something about the lady's personality. She appears calm, gentle, and forthright, not because of any action, emotion, or symbol, but because of Ghirlandaio's honesty, his concern with the careful representation of visible reality.

57

GIULIANO BUGIARDINI

b. Florence, 1475
d. Florence, 1554

Portrait of a Young Woman

Ca. 1516–20
Oil on panel
76.5 x 57.5 cm. (30 1/8 x 22 5/8 in.)
Inventory no. 27

Bugiardini represents the High Renaissance in Florence, with a style strongly influenced by his contemporary Raphael. Like various portraits by Raphael, ultimately derived from Leonardo's seminal *Mona Lisa*, Bugiardini's *Young Woman* is seen with her shoulders receding at an angle to the picture plane, so that her right shoulder is lower than her left. Her head turns to counterbalance this movement, and thus she is seen almost full-face. Again like its prototypes by Leonardo and by Raphael, Bugiardini's *Young Woman* is shown to below the waist, whereas earlier portraits were traditionally bust-length (such as Pisanello's medal, page 51). By extending the figure, the artist is able to include the sitter's expressive hand, which she presses to her breast, although what exactly this eloquent gesture may mean is difficult to say. The woman's gesture, her costume, and indeed her type of beauty all derive from Raphael's portrait *La Velata* (Pitti Palace, Florence), dated 1516. Raphael also employed a similar gesture, coiffure, and turban headdress for his nude *La Fornarina* (Galleria Nazionale, Rome).

Bugiardini's smooth contours and the largeness of his forms are characteristics of the Florentine High Renaissance style. The changing colors of the *Young Woman*'s gown, shifting from red to blue, are a device for modelling much favored by contemporary Mannerists, and her flesh is strongly shadowed with Leonardesque chiaroscuro.

58

59

GIOVANNI BATTISTA CIMA DA CONEGLIANO

b. Conegliano, 1459
d. Conegliano, 1518

Sacra Conversazione
(Rest on the Flight into Egypt)

Ca. 1500
Tempera and oil(?) on panel
53.9 x 71.6 cm. (21 1/4 x 28 3/16 in.)
Inventory no. 77

Cima's *Sacra Conversazione* is set in an expansive mountain landscape, evoking his native city of Conegliano (on the mainland near Venice), suffused with light and air, and permeated with a sense of the harmonious existence of man in nature. The Madonna is enthroned, so to speak, on a platform of rocks. Above her, a tree punctuates her central position and suggests the canopy of an earthly monarch's throne. Thus Cima represents at once two apparently contradictory themes: the Virgin enthroned as Queen of Heaven and also as the Madonna of Humility, seated upon the rocky ground. Graciously, and yet with an air of abstraction, Mary inclines her head to her right, toward St. John the Baptist with his cross. The saint closes the composition at the left by turning inward and pointing toward Christ, that is, identifying Him as the Lamb of God. Meanwhile, the Infant bends in the opposite direction, toward his left and St. Lucy, identified by her martyr's palm (in her left hand) and by her burning lamp.

Cima's famous altarpiece, the *Madonna dell' Arancio* (Venice, Accademia), dating from the mid-1490s, is the prototype of his *Madonna* in the Gulbenkian collection. There are several significant changes, however. The vertical emphasis of the altarpiece is replaced in the Gulbenkian panel by the horizontal format favored by Venetian artists in the early sixteenth century, and suggests a date of around 1500. Moreover, in translating his compositional ideas from a large altarpiece to a small image for private devotion, Cima appropriately represented a more intimate scene of the Holy Family, in which Joseph appears with Mary and the Child, rather than in the background. Such a representation of the complete group very likely appealed to the personal piety of the private household for which Cima would have painted this image.

61

VITTORE CARPACCIO

b. Venice, 1460/65
d. Venice, ca. 1526

Virgin and Child with Donors

Signed and dated: *VICTOR/*
CARPATHIVS/MDV
Tempera and oil(?) on panel
90.1 x 133.9 cm. (35 1/2 x 52 3/4 in.)
Inventory no. 208

Like his contemporary and compatriot Cima (page 61), the Venetian master Vittore Carpaccio also used a tranquil landscape as the setting for a sacred subject. A greatly skilled narrative painter, perhaps most famous for his cycles of St. Ursula and St. George, Carpaccio has interpreted this devotional image with picturesque anecdotal details. Riding in the middle distance are the Magi and part of their procession, coming to worship the newborn Christ Child. In order to emphasize the landscape setting, Carpaccio has moved the Holy Family out of the manger, of which only part of the roof is visible at the left. There too is one of its inhabitants, a donkey, whose head is partly seen, peeking out at the viewer. The donkey is frequently included in Nativity scenes to represent the Old Law that does not recognize the New, embodied in Christ.

Joseph sits next to the donkey and seems not to be fully aware of the new Infant. In this way, and by setting Joseph somewhat apart from the Virgin and Child, Carpaccio characterizes the old saint as the least significant member of the Holy Family—a distinction common to much Medieval and Renaissance art, including the *Sacra Conversazione* by Cima. But next to the praying Madonna is a bull, the symbol of the newly converted, represented with Mary as a cognizant worshipper of Christ. The baby lies on Mary's mantle on the ground and exchanges a meaningful glance with his mother, which associates them more closely with each other. To the left, the Child is adored by a gentleman and his wife, who take the place of the Magi, as it were. These are the donors, wearing the very rich and elegant garments of the early sixteenth-century Venetian upper class, but represented in the same space and in the same scale as Mary and Joseph. In short, the donors are depicted as though truly present at the scene of Christ's birth. Carpaccio's painting was undoubtedly commissioned by this couple for their private devotions. By being portrayed in the company of the Holy Family as Christ's first worshippers, the donors have expressed their personal faith as recommended by such medieval pious writings as the popular *Meditation on the Life of Christ*, which urges the worshipper to imagine himself actually in the presence of Mary, Christ, and the saints, sharing their experiences and their emotions. By signing his name and date on the *cartellino* (the illusionistic paper scroll near the Christ Child), Carpaccio attests to the artist's role in making visible this personal piety.

63

AFTER GIULIO ROMANO

b. Rome, 1499
d. Mantua, 1546

Fishing, from the series Children Playing

Ca. 1540
Tapestry: wool and silk with silver
  and gold threads
350 x 370 cm. (137 3/4 x 145 5/8 in.)
Inventory no. 29D

Giulio Romano, Raphael's close associate, was the highly esteemed court artist of the Gonzagas, the ruling family of Mantua. He was an architect, a painter, and also a tapestry designer, creating compositions for a series of *Children Playing*, of which three panels are exhibited in the Gulbenkian Museum. The tapestries resemble paintings in style, composition, and subject—pictures woven of wool, silk, and costly threads of silver and gold. Indeed, the high value of the materials is an important aspect of the aesthetic appeal and prestige of such tapestries.

The *Children* tapestries bear at the top the arms of Cardinal Ercole Gonzaga, the brother of Giulio's noble patron, the Duke of Mantua. In the panel seen here, a group of playful *amorini* or cupids amuse themselves in a grape arbor. Some climb and hover among the fruit, some eat greedily, some hide behind trellises and tree trunks, and others are fishing. Rolling hills and ancient ruins provide the setting. In a general way, the subject may be understood as a whimsical revival of classical antiquity, but the more immediate ancestors of Giulio's *amorini* are the spontaneous and playful cherubs in a ceiling fresco in the Ducal Palace at Mantua by Andrea Mantegna, Giulio's predecessor at the court. The gently provocative mood of Giulio's *amorini*, their suggestive poses, and the homoerotic behavior of the reclining couple at the right also recall Titian's canvas for Alfonso d'Este of Ferrara, entitled *The Worship of Venus*, painted in 1518–19. The Este and Gonzaga families were closely related by marriage; Cardinal Ercole Gonzaga's mother was the redoubtable Isabella d'Este, Alfonso d'Este's sister and his rival in art patronage. It is likely that Cardinal Ercole's tapestry commission was in part inspired by a friendly sense of competition between the two noble families.

JAN GOSSAERT *called* MABUSE

b. Maubeuge, ca. 1478
d. Breda, 1532

Nursing Madonna and Child

Ca. 1530
Oil on panel
78 x 54 cm. (30 3/4 x 21 1/4 in.)
Inventory no. 275

Jan Gossaert, the Netherlandish artist of the Court of Burgundy, signed his works as Joannes Malbodius (Mabuse), referring to his native city. The Madonna and Child was a favorite theme of the master, one he represented often and in a variety of ways. Here, a very muscular Child sits with legs crossed on his mother's lap and turns to grasp her breast to nurse. Mary looks down at the infant with wistful eyes, the tilt of her head suggesting tender affection. While the Child is in profile, the Madonna is frontal and shown seated, with the figure concealed below the knees by an elaborate architectural framework. In the foreground, the ledge is covered by an Oriental rug, on which Mary has set her Bible while nursing her baby. They are enclosed by an arch decorated on the piers with fictive sculptures of infants on pedestals. These crouching babies represent the first martyrs for Christ, the Innocents, slaughtered by order of King Herod. Above, the arch supports statuettes of Old Testament prophets who look down toward the Madonna and Child. The frontal plane of the arch is flush with the picture plane, so that the illusionistic architecture functions as a frame that brings the Virgin and Child very close to the viewer or worshipper. The architecture continues behind the Madonna, forming a vaulted canopy above her and opening to reveal a landscape vista, with a low palace, hills, and sky. Mabuse had been to Italy during 1508–09, and the strong influence of Italian Renaissance art on his work is especially evident in this landscape background. The minute scale of the distant forms as well as the delicate tracery and sculptural decoration are juxtaposed with the monumental figures of the Madonna and Child, enhancing their grandeur by contrast. The elaborate folds of Mary's red mantle and white veil have taken on an expressive life of their own. Not limited to reflecting the body, the draperies bend and swirl, enlivening the figure, and endowing Mary with a dramatic tension, conveying perhaps the Mother's fears for her infant's future, foreshadowed by the Massacre of the Innocents, who seem to watch over the Virgin and Child.

67

FRANS HALS

b. Antwerp, ca. 1580
d. Haarlem, 1666

Portrait of Sara Andriesdr. Hessix

1626
Oil on canvas
87 x 70 cm. (34 1/4 x 27 9/16 in.)
Inventory no. 214

In 1626, the great Dutch portraitist Frans Hals portrayed Sara Andriesdr. Hessix and her husband, the pastor Michiel Jansz. van Middelhoven, on the occasion of their fortieth anniversary. The pendant portrait of Middelhoven was lost in Paris during the Second World War, and its present whereabouts are unknown. Like her husband in the lost pendant, Sara is seated and holds a book, presumably the Bible, in her left hand. Her right hand is pressed to her heart. The portrait is historically important as Hals's first life-size depiction of a seated woman, and the pose became the prototype for many of his later female portraits.

Hals has placed Sara in her dark garments against a sombre background, with no indication of a specific setting or any decorative details, except for the deep red chair. This color note is a stunning surpise, interrupting the dark tones of the painting and the deep shadow cast by Sara herself against the wall and chair. In such a setting, the lightest, brightest forms, perforce the glowing focal points of our attention, are Sara's expressive hands and her face, surrounded by her white ruff and cap.

Hals's handling of paint is revolutionary. The application of paint to canvas in individual, distinguishable strokes represents a new style in European art that culminated in nineteenth-century French Impressionism. Hals does not define forms by the traditional means of modelling. Rather, forms are constructed or implied by his brushstrokes. These individual strokes represent the objective visual reality of Sara Hessix's appearance and communicate a sense of her pulsating life. Hals has captured one moment of action and of emotion, and has fixed that moment without sacrificing its vivacious vigor by means of the pace and movement of his brushstrokes. Sara seems present before the spectator, actually alive, perhaps about to speak—in fact, she appears as aware of the viewer as the viewer is of her.

69

REMBRANDT

b. Leyden, 1606
d. Amsterdam, 1669

Portrait of an Old Man

Dated: *f. 1645*
Oil on canvas
128 x 112 cm. (50 3/8 x 44 1/16 in.)
Inventory no. 1489

Rembrandt is a masterful portrayer of the intangible, of man's spirit, his inner life. His pictorial language emphasizes the effects of chiaroscuro (light-dark modelling) both to construct his compositions and to convey his meaning. The use of rich color, such as the red, is here subjugated to the play of golden light and dark shadow. In the *Portrait of an Old Man*, the sitter's hands and face seem to glow from within, as though this light metaphorically and actually represents the man's inner being. At the same time the chiaroscuro expresses the mood of the portrait. The old man is at once immensely dignified and ineffably sad. He is completely absorbed in his own tragic reflections. But even though he does not invite the viewer's response overtly, the old man in fact compels both emotional involvement and visual attention. The magical effect of Rembrandt's chiaroscuro is achieved by his extraordinary handling of paint. His brushstrokes are few and remarkably varied, with the paint applied in layers, so that color and light are interwoven, emerging together from the depths. This is different in technique and in effect from Hals's brushstrokes, which are all essentially alike, and flicker on the surface of the canvas. Rembrandt's light, emanating from within, illuminates both physically and spiritually.

REMBRANDT

Alexander the Great
  (also called *Pallas Athena*)

1661
Oil on canvas
118 x 91 cm. (46 1/2 x 35 13/16 in.)
Inventory no. 1488

The identity of this superb late work by Rembrandt has been disputed, although there is general agreement that the model was the artist's son Titus. The figure wears a fantastic helmet decorated with an owl, and holds a shield with the head of Medusa. These are traditional attributes of the Goddess of Wisdom, Pallas Athena. However, it seems almost certain that Rembrandt has represented *Alexander the Great*. The attributes associated with Athena are also found in ancient coins depicting Alexander who, moreover, is generally represented with long locks of hair, as in Rembrandt's portrayal. Most important in solving the question of the painting's subject, however, is the documentary evidence. In 1653 Rembrandt had painted *Aristotle Contemplating the Bust of Homer* (now in the Metropolitan Museum of Art, New York) for Count Antonio Ruffo. The *Aristotle* became the first of three paintings Rembrandt created for Ruffo to form a classical cycle: *Aristotle*; *Homer*, whose works Aristotle had explicated; and *Alexander the Great*, Aristotle's pupil. In 1661 an *Alexander* was sent to Count Ruffo, followed in 1663 by the *Homer* (now in the Mauritshuis, the Hague). But the Count was displeased with that *Alexander* (evidently the canvas now in the Art Gallery of Glasgow). The Gulbenkian *Alexander* may be recognized as Rembrandt's second version, which did indeed satisfy his noble patron.

In this work Rembrandt has combined the intense red of the drapery and plumes with the gold of the armor, in which the red appears yet again, in reflections. The helmet shadows Alexander's eyes, so that their expression is partially hidden. The spectator therefore must collaborate with Rembrandt in the definition of Alexander's mood and emotions and in so doing, becomes psychologically involved with the image. The extraordinary freedom and variation of Rembrandt's brushwork enlivens the surface and animates even the voids, endowing the entire surface with expressive power.

73

PETER PAUL RUBENS

b. Siegen, Westphalia, 1577
d. Antwerp, 1640

Portrait of Hélène Fourment

Ca. 1630–35
Oil on panel
186 x 86 cm. (73 1/4 x 33 7/8 in.)
Inventory no. 959

Rubens, the great leader of the Flemish school of painting in the seventeenth century, was also a successful diplomat, widely travelled, world-famous. His own cosmopolitan, aristocratic character is reflected in this splendid portrait of his second wife, Hélène Fourment. Rubens married Hélène in 1630, when she was only sixteen and the master fifty-three years of age. Rubens's portrait expresses his love for his young wife with great exuberance and *joie de vivre*. This is a profoundly sensuous image of the young woman—all luscious flesh, rich fabrics, glowing jewels, fluttering feathers. Hélène stands full-length in the foreground of an outdoor setting, completely dominating the composition. Her large dark eyes look at the spectator—or perhaps more accurately, at Rubens himself, as he paints her. She seems just to have turned toward us and begun to smile. Hélène's palpable physical and emotional closeness make this an intimate, ravishing portrait. Rubens's painterly handling, the remarkable fluidity of his strokes of color and light, animate the picture surface and indeed present Hélène to us, tangible and radiant.

75

PETER PAUL RUBENS

Flight into Egypt

Ca. 1630–32
Oil on panel
48.4 x 64 cm. (19 1/8 x 25 3/16 in.)
Inventory no. 78

Previously considered to be an oil sketch for the *Flight into Egypt* painted by Rubens in 1614, this painting is now recognized as a more mature reworking of that subject and composition. The Madonna, wearing a red gown, lovingly and protectively clasps the tiny Infant Christ to her breast, while turning back toward the angels above her as though for assurance, as they bring clouds to help conceal the Holy Family from their enemies, barely visible in the distance. Two other angels lead Mary's donkey and help guide the way to safety. St. Joseph follows and gestures toward the Mother and Son with tender solicitude. Rubens represents the *Flight into Egypt* as a poetic nocturne, with greyish underpainting to imply nighttime. The major source of illumination is the crescent moon, reflected below in the water.

This oil sketch, or *bozzetto*, is characterized by a remarkable freedom of handling that implies rapid, fluid execution. The spontaneous quality suggests that the artist worked quickly as his hand followed the inspiration of his mind. Vicariously, the spectator may experience the excitement of artistic creation as he views Rubens's dazzling *bozzetto*.

ANTHONY VAN DYCK

b. Antwerp, 1599
d. London, 1641

Portrait of a Man

Ca. 1626
Oil on canvas
142 x 112 cm. (55 7/8 x 44 1/8 in.)
Inventory no. 113

The portraits of Anthony van Dyck, the greatest of Rubens's associates, represent refined, elegant, confident individuals in a natural, spontaneous manner. The *Portrait of a Man* (previously and incorrectly identified as Anton or Nicolas Triest) was almost certainly painted in Italy around 1626 and illustrates the influence of Italian art, especially the Venetian, on Van Dyck's style.

The gentleman stands before a monumental stairway with grand columns. The background opens to a distant vista and sky. He is completely at ease, one hand resting on the back of a chair, the other free at his side. He wears the dark colors favored in the 1620s, but Van Dyck has embellished the garments by emphasizing the light reflected on the fabric. The tilt of the man's head, the turn of his eyes, the hint of a witty smile—all suggest his awareness of the spectator. It is a remarkably self-assured characterization, but not a pretentious one.

79

NICOLAS LANCRET

b. Paris,1690
d. Paris, 1745

Fête Galante

Ca. 1732
Oil on canvas
64.5 x 69.5 cm. (25 3/8 x 27 3/8 in.)
Inventory no. 958

The ancestry of the *fête galante* may be traced to the Venetian Renaissance master Giorgione, and its influence may be seen in the nineteenth-century French Impressionist representations of contemporaries at ease in natural landscape settings. But what distinguishes the *fête galante* from its origins and from its descendants is its specific relationship to the theater. In these scenes, eighteenth-century French ladies and gentlemen amuse themselves and each other with music and dancing, with flirtation and lovemaking. And they often do not appear as themselves but playfully assume the roles of shepherds and shepherdesses, or of traditional characters from the *commedia dell'arte*. The costume and scene designer Claude Gillot introduced the *fête galante* to painting, and his friend Antoine Watteau became the first master to be received into the Académie Royale as a painter of the genre. In 1719, Nicolas Lancret followed his master Watteau in this distinction.

Lancret's *fêtes* are at once more earthbound than Watteau's and less bittersweet in their representation of ephemeral pleasures. Lancret's elegant individuals are insouciant and gay, and completely untroubled by the realization that their dream must end. A luxuriant park provides the setting for their amusements, the dense leaves opening to admit a warm light that suffuses the atmosphere. Lancret applies thick touches of paint that make light and air palpable and reflect his direct observation of nature. Each figure is characterized as an individual, with distinctive poses, gestures, and expressions. All are united, however, by a lyrical mood of reverie. They behave as though enchanted, under a spell cast by Cupid. A discarded tambourine in the left foreground and the rhythmic arrangement of the figures suggest music and dancing, which now the ladies and gentlemen have abandoned, turning instead to amiable discourse and to seduction. Charmed and charming, Lancret's actors and their setting are at once real and unreal. They are eighteenth-century French men and women in an eighteenth-century French park—but their reality is perceived as a theatrical dream, a carefree suspension of everyday concerns and constraints.

81

FRANCOIS BOUCHER

b. Paris, 1703
d. Paris, 1770

Cupid and the Graces

Signed and dated: *F. Boucher/1738*
Oil on canvas
141 x 181 cm. (55 1/2 x 71 1/4 in.)
Inventory no. 433

François Boucher enjoyed great success and the highest patronage: encouraged by Madame de Pompadour, the artist rose to become both *Premier Peintre du Roi* (First Painter to the King) and director of the Tapestry Manufactory at Beauvais (see pages 84–85). Boucher's art was strongly influenced by Renaissance and contemporary Venetian masters, and admirers acknowledged this, complimenting him as the "Tiepolo of Paris."

Boucher painted an earlier version of *Cupid and the Graces* for the Princesse de Soubise, and that canvas can still be seen in its original location in the Hôtel de Soubise (now the Archives Nationales) in Paris, set above a doorway in the *Chambre de parade de la princesse*. The work was much appreciated and, having exhibited the canvas in the 1738 Salon, Boucher repeated the composition several times: in the painting now in the Gulbenkian collection; in an engraving; and, in 1754, in a variation for the boudoir of Madame de Pompadour.

For Boucher and for his patrons, mythological subjects seem to have been merely the pretext for the representation of scenes intended to delight and to appeal to the senses. One of the Graces in this life-size painting binds little Cupid with chains of flowers, while her sisters look on. But Boucher's true subject is the representation of enticing female nudes with creamy flesh in provocative poses on cushions of clouds.

Although unarmed, Cupid is not seriously endangered by his voluptuous captors. Their mood is completely playful and carefree. Diderot, Boucher's contemporary and the author of the *Encyclopédie*, deplored this sensual gaiety, complaining that such art lacked both propriety and morality. To be sure, Diderot's hostile criticism is accurate—and, ironically, one may agree with him while yet appreciating Boucher's art as the embodiment of enjoyment and pleasure.

82

83

AFTER FRANCOIS BOUCHER

Jupiter with Grapes

Mid-eighteenth century
Tapestry: wool and silk
365 x 280 cm. (143¾ x 110¼ in.)
Inventory no. 281

84

The art of François Boucher—gay, sensuous, and exuberant—typifies the extravagant Rococo style of the reign of Louis XV. Between 1736 and 1752, Boucher designed six series of tapestries of exquisite quality and elegance for the great tapestry manufactory of Beauvais. *Jupiter with Grapes* is the fourth panel from the series, *The Loves of the Gods*. The antique characters do not serve any particular narrative purpose. Rather, the theme and composition are similar to many painted works by Boucher, in which a classical subject is the excuse for presenting beautiful women in revealing garments and suggestive poses. Boucher evokes sensory pleasure—the taste and aroma of ripe fruits, the sounds of music, the feeling of sunlight on soft flesh.

AFTER FRANCOIS BOUCHER

The Bird Catchers

Signed and dated: *F. Boucher, 1755*
Tapestry: wool and silk
348 x 588 cm. (137 x 231 ½ in.)
Inventory no. 280

The Bird Catchers is a panel from the last tapestry series Boucher designed for Beauvais, called *La Noble Pastorale* or *Les Beaux Pastorales*. The figures wear contemporary eighteenth-century French garments, but the ruins suggest the antique past, especially the round temple, which alludes to the famous Roman Temple of the Sibyl at Tivoli. Boucher's elegant ladies and gentlemen amuse themselves by trapping songbirds in the net at the right, and caging them as pets. This activity is apparently innocent, but Boucher's interpretation is seductive: the lackadaisical mood of the young people, their intertwined poses and lingering glances, suggest that catching birds is merely a masquerade, barely concealing the amorous intent that unites them.

85

JEAN HENRI RIESENER

b. Gladbeck, Westphalia, 1734
d. Paris, 1806

Rolltop Desk

Stamped: *J.H. Riesener*
1773
Various woods with ormolu
110 x 58 x 105 cm. (43 1/4 x 22 7/8 x
41 3/8 in.)
Inventory no. 2082

Jean Henri Riesener was both the principal *ébéniste* (cabinet-maker) of the French royal family and the greatest furniture maker of the eighteenth century. In 1760, J. F. Oeben had been commissioned to make a desk for Louis XV, which was completed by his pupil Riesener in 1769 and signed by Riesener alone. That rolltop desk, now in the Louvre, became the starting point for the new Louis XVI style, in which gilt mounts underscore the architectural structure of the piece. Versions of the king's desk were made for various members of the royal family, including the Gulbenkian bureau, seen here, signed by Riesener. This bureau once furnished the Versailles apartments of the Comtesse de Provence, wife of the man who would have ruled as Louis XVII.

Every surface of the bureau is embellished with *trompe-l'oeil* designs. Its cylindrical lid is made of separate slats of wood. Closed, the top reveals an illusionistic design in marquetry, representing flowers, books, quill pens in an inkwell, and various attributes of music. When opened, of course, the top disappears into the body of the desk. The other surfaces are decorated with marquetry fruits and flowers whose naturalistic shading is achieved by subtle variations in color and tone of the woods used. Elaborate bronze mounts with swirling foliate motifs adorn the front drawer and the cabriole legs, which end in clawed feet. The upper surface of the desk is surrounded at the sides and back by a balustrade with two consoles bearing double candlesticks. All of these intricate and sumptuous ormolu fittings were probably designed by Riesener himself. His superb *bureau à cylindre* is the epitome of French eighteenth-century *douceur de vivre*.

MARTIN CARLIN

b. Freiburg im Breisgau, Germany,
  ca. 1730
d. Paris, 1785

Writing Table

Stamped: *M. Carlin*
Ca. 1771
Various woods with ormolu and
  Sèvres porcelain
73 x 36 x 63 cm. (28 3/4 x 14 3/16 x
  24 3/4 in.)
Inventory no. 2267

The *ébéniste* Martin Carlin specialized in magnificient furniture set with plaques of Sèvres porcelain. This dazzling *table en auge*, or trough-shaped table, was most likely ordered by the Parisian *marchand-mercier* Poirier for Queen Marie-Antoinette, who presented it to her sister, Queen Maria Carolina of Naples.

The table is embellished with richly colored plaques of Sèvres porcelain secured by narrow frames of gilded bronze, or ormolu. The central oval plaque is signed by the porcelain painter Dodin and dated 1771. The table also bears the signature of Carlin. A low gallery around the back and sides acts as a barrier to prevent objects from falling off the top. Lavish ormolu fittings decorate the table, including the lock of the central drawer in the front. The fluted legs are slender and tapered. Every surface is elaborate, lustrous, richly painted. Carlin's mastery makes the table a precious decorative object—functional, to be sure, but with its practical purpose merely the point of departure for an exquisite Rococo fantasy.

89

JEAN HONORE FRAGONARD

b. Grasse, 1732
d. Paris, 1806

The Island of Love
(The Fête at Rambouillet)

Ca. 1780
Oil on canvas
71 x 90 cm. (28 x 35 1/2 in.)
Inventory no. 436

Fragonard studied with François Boucher and, like his master, represented scenes of sensual pleasure, generally untroubled by moral implications or by the transience of such experience. *The Island of Love* was exhibited in 1782 in the Salon de la Correspondance, and described as "A grotto decorated with architecture, with figures." It has variously been suggested that the delightful landscape and elegant pleasure-seekers represent a *fête* at Rambouillet, a residence of Marie-Antoinette's friend the Princesse de Lamballe; a *fête* given in 1782 at Chantilly by the Prince de Condé for the Archduke and Archduchess of Russia; or a *fête* given by Bergeret de Grancourt, whom Fragonard frequently visited. But the identity of the event is less important than the evocation of a charmed existence dedicated to love and gaiety. Fragonard differs from his teacher Boucher in representing these themes with contemporary scenes and characters, rather than the classical heroes of mythology. His art is the visual expression of the capriciousness, insouciance, and erotic sensuality of the French aristocracy before the Revolution.

Fragonard's style is also unlike that of Boucher, being freer and sketchier. Landscape interested Fragonard greatly, and in *The Island of Love* the landscape setting with rushing water is a protagonist no less important than the figures themselves in the creation of a passionate, idyllic mood.

91

FRANCOIS THOMAS GERMAIN

b. Paris, 1726
d. Paris, 1791

Centerpiece

Ca. 1766
Silver
Three pieces: center, 53.5 x 67 cm. (21 1/16 x
  26 3/8 in.); sides, 41 x 33 cm. (16 1/8 x 13 in.)
Inventory no. 1085A/B/C

Of the various branches of the decorative arts, perhaps the goldsmith's craft best reflects the taste and culture of a particular society. While functional, the mid-eighteenth-century works shown here illustrate the ornate *rocaille* style and sophisticated technique of the reign of Louis XV. The term *rocaille* refers to the use of forms that are lively and charming, asymmetrical and often fantastic. The small cupids in this centerpiece are playing among bunches of grapes, like infant disciples of the god Bacchus. The theme is typical of French Rococo style, lyrical, diverting, and lighthearted.

François Thomas Germain took over his father's workshop as silversmith and sculptor to the King in 1748. He executed this piece for Czarina Elisabeth in commemoration of the victory of Prince Soltikof over Frederick II at Kunersdorf. She asked him to supply a centerpiece of Bacchus and Love as part of a complete service. The greater part of this "Paris Service" still exists in the Hermitage Museum.

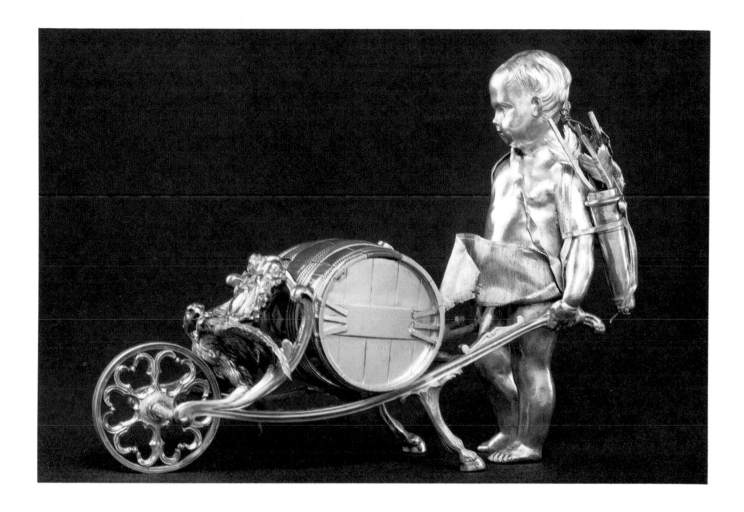

**ANTOINE SEBASTIEN
DURAND**

Place unknown, ca. 1710
Place unknown, 1785

Mustard Barrel

Eighteenth century
Silver
18 x 9 x 23 cm. (7 $\frac{1}{16}$ x 3 $\frac{1}{2}$ x
9 $\frac{1}{16}$ in.)
Inventory no. 287

 Only two extant decorative table pieces are known to have been owned by Mme de Pompadour—a pair of gravy boats now in the Musée des Arts Decoratifs, Paris, and a pair of mustard pots, one of which is shown here. The pots were executed by Antoine Sebastien Durand, a master goldsmith of Paris who excelled in creating plant and wave forms as well as figures of pert, graceful childhood. The eighteenth century loved juvenile grace and Durand often used it as his theme. Mme de Pompadour, who commissioned these pieces from Durand, was the principal mistress of Louis XV from 1745 until her death in 1764. Her expenditures during that time were phenomenal, but she had an eye for art and her taste was impeccable.

HUBERT ROBERT

b. Paris, 1733
d. Paris, 1808

***Felling the Trees at Versailles:
The Baths of Apollo***

Ca. 1775
Oil on canvas
67 x 101.7 cm. (26 3/8 x 40 in.)
Inventory no. 627

Writing in 1775 in his *Mémoire*, Hubert Robert described this scene: "The point of view . . . is taken from the Baths of Apollo, of which one sees in the right foreground one of the groups of horses; the palace is in the background. . . ." Robert refers to the garden facade of the palace of Versailles, with the marble sculpture *Tritons with the Horses of Apollo*, one of two groups that flanked an artificial rock and grotto in Robert's new landscaping design for the Royal Gardens. Like its pendant on the opposite page, this canvas records the destruction of Le Nôtre's austere, geometric landscaping, preliminary to Robert's picturesque and romantic recreation of the distant past of classical antiquity.

While workmen chop and saw the trees, members of the court watch in the incongruous surroundings of rubble and debris, and in the silent company of Neoclassical marbles.

HUBERT ROBERT

Felling the Trees at Versailles:
The Greensward

Ca. 1775
Oil on canvas
67 x 101.7 cm. (26 ⅜ x 40 in.)
Inventory no. 626

Like his great predecessor Claude Lorrain, Robert was devoted to the scenery and ancient monuments of Italy. His art is poetic and evocative, a visual reverie about times long past. His predilection for such scenes reflects a widespread fascination for ancient Rome in the eighteenth century. This taste for antiquity, an intoxication with the past, led to the extensive remodellings of the Royal Gardens at Versailles, where Robert was able to translate his archeological fantasies from canvas to reality, as Designer of the King's Gardens, beginning in 1778. Here the artist has recorded the felling of the trees at Versailles. Robert juxtaposes the felling of the trees with the great stone recreations of classical subjects and monuments, and sets the rough workmen in the elegant company of ladies and gentlemen of the court.

95

MAURICE QUENTIN DE LA TOUR

b. St.-Quentin, 1704
d. St.-Quentin, 1788

Portrait of Duval de l'Epinoy

1745
Pastel
119.5 x 92.8 cm. (47 x 36 1/2 in.)
Inventory no. 2380

Quentin de La Tour worked exclusively in pastel, a medium associated in modern times with casual sketches, but which the eighteenth-century French master handled with dazzling refinement and grandeur. La Tour required many sittings of his subjects and made numerous preparatory studies before producing the finished work. One study for this portrait of Duval de l'Epinoy is known, preserved in a private collection in Paris. The nobleman Duval was the secretary to Louis XV and evidently also personally close to the monarch, for the King acted as witness at the marriage of Duval's second daughter in 1753. La Tour portrayed other members of the royal court, including the King and Queen themselves, and beginning in 1745, the date of Duval's portrait, was given lodgings at the Louvre.

Duval is seen in his study, seated at his desk. A globe, shelves of books, and a large open volume suggest his erudition and intellectual interests. He has interrupted his reading, however, as though in response to the spectator, who is conceived as a visitor. Duval smiles, perhaps with a suggestion of hauteur, and seems about to take snuff from a gleaming box in his hands. The portrait is presented as a precious object, in part as a result of the costly opulence of the splendid things represented—the snuff box, the lace and shimmering moiré silk of the garments, the elegant powdered wig, Duval's gilded chair with rich red fabric, the carved desk, even the tooled leather bindings of the books. But the splendor of the portrait is not expressed only by expensive and sumptuous objects—it is conveyed by Duval himself, whose extraordinary elegance and refinement are inherent in his character. This brilliant portrait has always been recognized as La Tour's masterpiece: as the critic Mariette wrote in the *Livret* of the 1745 Salon where the work was exhibited, "*C'est le triomphe de la peinture au pastel* (It is the triumph of painting in pastel)."

97

THOMAS GAINSBOROUGH

b. Sudbury, Suffolk, 1727
d. London, 1788

Portrait of Mrs. Lowndes-Stone

1775
Oil on canvas
232 x 153 cm. (91 3/8 x 60 1/4 in.)
Inventory no. 429

Thomas Gainsborough probably painted Mrs. Lowndes-Stone in 1775, on the occasion of her marriage. Gainsborough's portraiture was strongly influenced by Van Dyck's in style and in conception. Mrs. Lowndes-Stone is depicted with the refinement, elegance, and self-assurance of Van Dyck's ladies and gentlemen. To these qualities Gainsborough has added his own charming informality and tranquil lyricism. Mrs. Lowndes-Stone is shown walking with her lively dog in a peaceful, airy landscape setting. Gainsborough's light, fluent brushstrokes capture her movement and evoke the soft rustling of her silk and lace gown, shimmering in the sunlight. The artist's treatment of atmosphere, landscape, rich fabrics, and even the dog is suggestive, free, and painterly. However, his handling of paint in the representation of Mrs. Lowndes-Stone's face is more formal and precise—after all, this is a portrait, intended as an accurate depiction of the lady's appearance. As for her character, Gainsborough has interpreted this with his own customary grace. Mrs. Lowndes-Stone's mood is a happy one—she turns to smile gently at the viewer, and naturally the viewer wishes to smile in return.

GEORGE ROMNEY

b. Dalton-in-Furness, Lancashire,
    1734
d. Kendal, Westmorland, 1802

Portrait of Miss Constable

1787
Oil on canvas
76 x 64 cm. (30 x 25 3/16 in.)
Inventory no. 427

Miss Constable sat six times for George Romney during May and June of 1787, and her portrait was sent in July to William Morwood, Esq., of Yorkshire. Thus Romney completed his work rather quickly, and this may be reflected in the freshness and immediacy of his portrayal. The composition is pleasantly informal: Miss Constable sits sideways in the foreground and turns toward the spectator. It is also boldly asymmetrical, and the sitter's torso, hair, and angled hat form varied patterns against the ground. The hat, casually decorated with wheat, and Miss Constable's long free hair enframe her face, which is the most highly finished part of the painting. Elsewhere, especially in the dress, Romney models more broadly, and perhaps the skirt and left sleeve were left unfinished. Miss Constable's hair, eyes, and lips are the most strongly colored areas of the portrait, and this too emphasizes the primary importance of the face. She is completely and naturally at ease, with her hands on her lap and hidden from view, so that they cannot contend with her face for attention. Miss Constable's expression is calm and dignified, and she smiles gently as she looks toward the spectator. The freshness and simplicity of Romney's composition and the freedom of his handling of paint characterize the young lady as quietly assured, charming, and unpretentious, and establish a straightforward, amiable association between the viewer and Miss Constable.

THOMAS LAWRENCE

b. Bristol, 1769
d. London, 1830

Portrait of Lady Elizabeth Conyngham

1824
Oil on canvas
142.9 x 111.2 cm. (56 1/4 x 43 3/4 in.)
Inventory no. 2360

Sir Thomas Lawrence had a brilliant career. He began painting as a child prodigy; in 1792 he succeeded Sir Joshua Reynolds as Painter to the King, and was himself knighted in 1815; and in 1820 he became President of the Royal Academy. A list of Lawrence's portraits is tantamount to an index of the most powerful and socially prominent figures of his time, and in 1815, following the defeat of Napoleon, the recently knighted portraitist embarked on an artistic campaign to portray England's allies, including the Emperors of Austria and of Russia. *Lady Elizabeth*, later Marchioness of Huntly, epitomizes Lawrence's society portraits, and especially his romantic, fashionable representations of women.

Lawrence was an ardent devotee of the theater, and a certain theatricality permeates his characterization of *Lady Elizabeth*. The portrait is virtually staged rather than naturalistically posed. Lady Elizabeth, exquisitely costumed and bejewelled, sits in the central foreground of a garden setting, holding an elaborately carved and inlaid harp. Her coiffure and maquillage are glamourous and stylish. Her smile and the tilt of her head on a very long, cylindrical neck suggest flirtatious sophistication. This is hardly a portrait that pretends to be an unplanned confrontation between sitter and spectator. Lady Elizabeth's audience, the viewer, is not to forget that she is striking a pose. The composition and conception of the portrait are insistently artificial—a most unlikely combination of elegant drawing-room formality (complete with musical prop) and a garden setting, illuminated as though by spotlight. Yet despite this staginess, the portrait is persuasive: Lawrence, believing enthusiastically in the poetic "romance of woman," dazzles and convinces his audience. Lady Elizabeth's sheer gown, shimmering jewels, and even her harp are carefully conceived as projections of her character. This was the age of Beau Brummel, a time of extraordinary obsession with the importance of modish appearance; Lawrence shared that obsession. His rich colors, flowing lines, and stylish characterization represent the glittering extravagance, luxurious comfort, and unquestioned security of Lady Elizabeth Conyngham's existence.

103

JEAN ANTOINE HOUDON

b. Versailles, 1741
d. Paris, 1828

Diana

Signed and dated: *J. A. Houdon 1780*
Marble
210 cm. high (82 $^{11}/_{16}$ in.)
Inventory no. 1390

The marble *Diana*—a masterpiece of eighteenth-century European sculpture—was ironically commissioned as a consolation to Houdon, when his project for the chapel of the mother of Duke Ernest II of Saxe-Gotha was rejected. In a mollifying gesture of *noblesse oblige*, the Duke ordered a garden sculpture of Diana, and Houdon completed a plaster cast of the goddess in 1776 (now in the Schlossmuseum, Gotha). However, it was not until 1780 that the master signed and dated the marble *Diana* now in the Gulbenkian Museum. The subject and its conception fascinated both the artist and his public, and Houdon produced three additional versions of *Diana*, two cast in bronze, dated 1782 and 1790, and a terracotta, modelled around 1778. The marble *Diana*, although paid for by Duke Ernest, could not be safely delivered because of war, and was resold instead to Catherine the Great of Russia. It is one of Gulbenkian's purchases from the Hermitage. The Duke had to be satisfied with the plaster cast.

The theme of Diana, the virgin huntress and moon goddess, had been popular in classical antiquity and had been revived during the Renaissance, so that the subject was quite familiar in the eighteenth century. But Houdon's interpretation of it is extraordinary in two ways: the goddess is nude, and she is in motion. Previously, Diana the huntress was traditionally clothed, while the nude Diana was represented as a reclining figure. Consequently, the nudity of Houdon's running figure startled contemporaries, and the physiological precision of her body shocked them. The sensuous carving evokes the smoothness of her flesh, emphasized by contrast with her soft hair crowned by a crescent moon, the quiver of arrows, and the tall reeds next to her legs. Perhaps even more remarkable than *Diana*'s nudity is her movement. She is running, her weight entirely on the ball of one foot. The reeds, necessary as a support for the marble figure, suggest the scene of the hunt. *Diana* is to be appreciated completely in the round, from all viewpoints, and from any one of them she presents a different yet completely convincing vision of fleet action.

105

JEAN ANTOINE HOUDON

Apollo

1790
Bronze
213 cm. high (83 $^7/_8$ in.)
Inventory no. 552

Houdon's bronze *Apollo* is inscribed on the base with the date and the names of the artist and his patron: *Houdon F. 1790. Pour Jn. Girardot de Marigny, négociant à Paris.* Marigny owned the artist's bronze *Diana* done in 1782, which was similar to the Gulbenkian marble *Diana* pictured on the previous page. Around 1786, he commissioned the sculpture of the goddess's brother Apollo as a companion piece. In the next year, Houdon constructed his own bronze-casting foundry, and thus was both the sculptor and founder of the *Apollo* cast in 1788—a combination of skills of which he was justifiably proud. Although bronze casting permits the production of more than one sculpture from a single mold, the Gulbenkian *Apollo* is unique; no other casts are known to have been made.

Apollo is derived from one of the most famous and influential sculptures of classical antiquity, the *Apollo Belvedere*, now in the Vatican Museums. Like others before him, Houdon took the ancient model as both an inspiration and a challenge. He had already adapted the *Belvedere* in his own *Diana*. Like *Diana, Apollo* is shown explicitly nude, running and with his head turned to the right. Unlike the goddess, he is poised on the ball of his right foot. Because the sculpture is bronze and therefore hollow, the figure may be completely free-standing, independent of props such as the reeds necessary to support the marble *Diana*. The sensuality of his nudity, in particular the softness of his flesh, is comparable to *Diana's*: thus the two figures form a pair, despite their differing media.

Apollo's right arm is extended before him, and his left is at his side, holding a lyre, his attribute as god of music and poetry. As he runs, his hair is blown back by the wind, its rough texture juxtaposed with the smooth skin. The agitated movement of the hair suggests Apollo's speed as he runs, and contrasts with the unhurried, graceful rhythm of his body.

FRANCESCO GUARDI

b. Venice, 1712
d. Venice, 1793

The Feast of the Ascension in the Piazza San Marco

Ca. 1765–75
Oil on canvas
61 x 91 cm. (24 x 35 13/16 in.)
Inventory no. 390

Of all the *vedutisti*, or view painters of Venice, Francesco Guardi is perhaps the most lyrical, preoccupied more with the changing moods of the city than with its appearance. Guardi's views of Venice are visual poems about its ephemeral quality, the shimmering light, crepuscular air, glistening water.

The two views illustrated here form a set with two other canvases also in the Gulbenkian collection, all dating around 1775. Preparatory drawings for the two illustrated paintings are in the British Museum, London.

In *The Feast of the Ascension in the Piazza San Marco*, Guardi takes the obvious vantage point in the Piazza opposite the Basilica of San Marco, but by standing somewhat to the side he emphasizes the Piazza's irregular trapezoidal shape. The Piazza has often been compared to a great open-air theater or drawing room, and Guardi exploits the dramatic and social features of his scene. Strong sunlight, interrupted by equally strong shadows, spotlights the casual procession of fashionable Venetians moving away from Guardi and the viewer toward the Basilica. Their movement is emphasized by the diagonals of the Piazza, with its special arcades built for the celebration of the feast, and by the diagonal of the dark shadow pointing like an arrow toward the church, gradually lightening until it reaches the luminous climax of the composition and of the figures' progress: the Basilica itself. Guardi invites the spectator to accompany these elegant worshippers: the viewer stands with the artist, behind the Venetian crowd, and their movement toward the Basilica suggests that we join them in celebration of the feast.

FRANCESCO GUARDI

The Regatta Seen from Ca' Foscari

Ca. 1765–75
Oil on canvas
61 x 91 cm. (24 x 35 7/8 in.)
Inventory no. 391

Guardi adapted this composition from a painting by Canaletto which had been engraved by Visentini in 1742. The palaces of the Grand Canal, with their characteristic chimneys and some with the obelisks signifying the residence of an admiral, form insistent diagonals plunging into the distance and coming to their resolution at the Rialto Bridge, barely visible on the horizon. As in the companion painting of *The Feast of the Ascension* on the previous page, the Venetians have turned away from the spectator, now to observe the regatta. However, while the open foreground of the Piazza allowed the viewer to believe that he too might enter the scene, here such an imaginary entrance is blocked in the foreground by gondolas waiting in a row parallel to the picture surface. These gondolas close the scene in the foreground just as the palaces create diagonal boundaries on the sides of the composition. These structures frame the Grand Canal, mostly unpopulated in the center, so that the water itself, with its muted reflections of color and light, becomes the focus of the spectator's attention. The horizon is low, as in *The Feast of the Ascension* and indeed as in the actual city of Venice. The master exploits this geographical fact to give over half his composition to the sky. Guardi's sky is empty of solid forms or action, but filled with an air that is richly colored and palpable, enlivened by the play of shifting light and color. Indeed, the sky and water of Venice are Guardi's protagonists, the regatta merely the excuse for his capturing the transitory magic of the city of the lagoons.

110

JOSEPH MALLORD WILLIAM TURNER

b. London, 1775
d. Chelsea, 1851

The Wreck of a Transport Ship

1810
Oil on canvas
173 x 245 cm. (68 1/8 x 96 1/2 in.)
Inventory no. 260

A constant theme in the oeuvre of J.M.W. Turner was the fearful and mighty power of violent nature, especially the sudden catastrophic force of fire or water. Turner's sketchbooks reveal his particular interest in representing stormy waters, and his having witnessed an impressive shipwreck in 1803 or 1804. This experience inspired the masterpiece that first revealed the full scope of Turner's genius, *The Shipwreck* of 1805 (the Tate Gallery, London). He returned to a similar subject and composition in 1810, in a canvas exhibited in his own gallery with the title *The Wreck of the "Minotaur,"* which was bought by the Hon. Charles Pelham, later the Earl of Yarborough. In 1849, the second Earl lent the masterpiece for exhibition at the British Institution, where it was displayed with its present title, *The Wreck of a Transport Ship*.

The particular narrative details of the subject are less important than the artist's conception of nature's tumultuous energy. The sea has become a violently swirling vortex that overpowers mere men. At the left, the great ship has turned on its side, its masts broken, vanquished by the storm. A few seamen still cling pathetically to the edge of the ship, silhouetted against the sky. The ship is the major dark form in the composition, dramatically juxtaposed with the brightest area, the central flash of light. The only strong color is the red of the uniforms of some of the crew who are being rescued by a small rowboat, itself in great danger. Other rescuers in fishing boats are likewise threatened by the sea. The English critic John Burnet, writing in 1850, described this painting with a quotation from Shakespeare's *Macbeth*: "the yeasty waves confounding and swallowing navigation up." And yet, Turner reminds us, although men may lose their lives in their struggle with nature, their heroic attempt to survive is magnificent.

113

JOSEPH MALLORD WILLIAM TURNER

Quilleboeuf, Mouth of the Seine

Ca. 1833
Oil on canvas
88 x 120 cm. (34 5/8 x 47 1/4 in.)
Inventory no. 2362

Turner exhibited this canvas at the Royal Academy in 1833 with the title and explanatory text, "*Mouth of the Seine, Quille-boeuf.* This estuary is so dangerous from its quicksands, that any vessel taking the ground is liable to be stranded and overwhelmed by the rising tide, which rushes in in one wave." In his earlier *Wreck of a Transport Ship*, pictured on the previous page, Turner had portrayed the actual struggle of man in nature. But here men themselves are insignificant, and their structures, mere stone and wood, are almost conquered by cosmic turmoil. Travel in Italy and the study of Titian's works had influenced the further development of Turner's technique and style, which became the expressive instruments of his Romantic subjects. This composition is dominated by the agitated sea and sky, their swirling motions repeated by the flying seagulls at the left. Atmosphere is palpable, as in works by such Venetian masters as Guardi, but in Turner it is excited and destructive, not peaceful and beneficent. And as in the Venetian paintings, here too atmosphere consumes solid structures, dissolving contours and uniting the composition in a chromatic miasma.

115

THEODORE ROUSSEAU

b. Paris, 1812
d. Barbizon, 1867

Autumnal Landscape

Signed: *Th. Rousseau*
Ca. 1840–49
Oil on panel
21.5 x 53.5 cm. (8 1/2 x 21 1/16 in.)
Inventory no. 453

Théodore Rousseau was already painting—and painting out of doors—in his teenage years. In 1836 he became the first artist to move to Barbizon, near the Fontainebleau Forest, and his studio there became a gathering place for other artists of the so-called Barbizon School, such as Millet. Rousseau uses energetic brushstrokes and strong colors to represent isolated rustic scenes. He requires no human or historical *raison d'être* for landscape, unlike earlier French masters such as Lancret or Robert. Landscape is not merely the setting of Rousseau's art—it is the protagonist.

The freedom with which Rousseau paints recalls for the viewer the actuality of being out of doors, and makes him in effect a witness to the artist's creative act. Rousseau's technique represents a culmination of the emergence of the oil sketch as a finished work of art.

Rousseau paints a scene with a very low horizon, so that the sky occupies approximately two-thirds of the picture space. A row of trees dominates the middle ground, some bending to the right, but one in the center proudly upright. They seem to be in communion. The land unfolds in horizontal planes, parallel with the painting's surface. A small pond reflects broken patches of color from the sky, trees, and a single figure in red, black, and white.

Rousseau wrote of his representations of trees as portraits of them. He, like Millet, understood nature in human terms. "See all those beautiful trees," he exclaimed. Lit by the sun, Rousseau explained, a tree becomes "a column which has muscles, limbs, hands, and a beautiful skin . . . Ah! the sun . . . it makes everything move, everything feel, everything attract."

117

JEAN FRANCOIS MILLET

b. Gruchy, France, 1814
d. Barbizon, 1875

The Rainbow

Signed: *J. F. Millet*
Ca. 1870
Pastel
42 x 54 cm. (16 1/2 x 21 1/4 in.)
Inventory no. 88

Beginning in 1849, Millet lived in Barbizon, where he was associated with Théodore Rousseau, whose work and ideas strongly influenced his own. Unlike Rousseau, however, Millet did not prepare studies directly from nature, much less paint finished pictures *en plein air*. Instead, he worked in his studio, basing his landscapes on recollection, not observation. Earlier in his career, he had depicted landscape scenes with hard-working peasants, and even after he had turned to the theme of pure landscape, he represented not wild nature but the land tamed and changed by human effort.

The Rainbow, a pastel that may be associated with an oil painting of the same title, dated 1873 and now in the Louvre, is such a scene, a landscape controlled by man for his own benefit. Even though the pastel would have been done in the studio, as was Millet's practice, his choppy strokes and dashes of color suggest the immediacy of direct vision. Individual strokes are densely interwoven, and the picture appears a tapestry of color and light. For Millet as for Rousseau, landscape scenes were animated visually by effects of air and sunlight, and spiritually by an emotional view of nature. Indeed, for both artists, trees were the living personnages of their compositions, beings, as Millet wrote, of "calmness, of ... grandeur.... I don't know what those fellows, the trees, are saying to each other; but they're saying something we don't understand, because we don't speak the same language." Perhaps not, and yet Millet's landscape is imbued with a feeling of sympathetic communion with the natural world.

119

CHARLES FRANCOIS DAUBIGNY

b. Paris, 1817
d. Paris, 1878

Portjoie Near Bonnières

Signed and dated: *Daubigny, 1865*
Oil on panel
27 x 49 cm. (10 5/8 x 19 1/4 in.)
Inventory no. 444

Of their generation, only Boudin and Daubigny both painted out of doors and actually finished their works *en plein air*. Daubigny shared many of the Impressionists' interests and ideas. For example, unlike his colleagues in Barbizon, he frequently preferred the theme of water to that of the forest. His primary concern was the accurate observation of changing light and atmosphere, and he fixed the immediacy of his vision with free, rapid brushstrokes. By applying paint to canvas with small daubs, Daubigny mimics the informality of an oil sketch. Forms are not defined with clearly drawn, linear contours, as in the past. That traditional artistic technique is abandoned, and forms exist only as dashes of color and light. Wishing to observe transient light in nature, Daubigny outfitted a small boat as a floating studio, called "Le Botin," and on this he must have painted the Gulbenkian landscape.

Portjoie Near Bonnières closely resembles the *Twilight* (*Crépuscule de Lune*) dated 1866 and exhibited in the Salon of the following year (now in the Walters Art Gallery, Baltimore). Daubigny used "Le Botin" on the river Oise for the last time in that same year, 1867. This working method, painting from a boat, was later emulated by Monet. "Le Botin" enabled Daubigny to stand completely surrounded by the reflected light and color of the water he was painting.

Although Daubigny thus resembled the Impressionists in his subjects and technique, he is unlike them in mood. He takes a more personal, sentimental view of nature, representing idyllic scenes that encourage tranquil contemplation and a feeling of poignant melancholy. His follower Frederic Henriet appreciated this aspect of his master's art: "The model is before his eyes, but it is in his heart that he finds the exquisite feeling with which he impregnates his work."

121

JEAN BAPTISTE CAMILLE COROT

b. Paris, 1796
d. Ville-d'Avray, 1875

View of Venice from the Dogana

Signed: *Corot*
1834
Oil on canvas
26 x 38 cm. (10¼ x 15 in.)
Inventory no. 442

The great French landscape painter Camille Corot visited Venice in August and September of 1834, and the aesthetic experience of that extraordinary city was seminal in his artistic development. Corot's vision of the city was inspired by the tradition of the Venetian view-painters, such as Guardi (pages 109 and 111).

Corot's vantage point was the *Dogana* (Customs House), looking across the Grand Canal toward the major monuments of the city center: from left to right, the Gardens of San Marco, the *Zecca* (Mint), the Library, the Columns of St. Theodore and St. Mark, the belltower and domes of the Basilica of San Marco, the Ducal palace, prisons, and the churches and palaces of the *Riva degli Schiavoni*. The canvas is marked on the back with the stamp of the Corot Sale, the sale of paintings still in the master's studio at his death, indicating that he never parted with this early work.

A lonely gondola, rowed diagonally toward San Marco, leads the viewer into the scene. Although the buildings and shoreline also recede toward the right, the diagonal recession is ultimately denied by Corot's emphasis on the planar surface of the canvas. In addition, the textured horizontal band of water does not recede, but asserts the surface over depth. Such emphasis on the surface is a primary characteristic of modern painting, as distinct from Renaissance and Baroque interest in pictorial depth.

To paint a view of Venice, with its buildings low in the horizon, is to paint its luminous sky and the reflecting water of its canals—compositions in which the artist is compelled to emphasize the ever-changing effects of illumination. Solid structures of churches and palaces are barely more substantial than the ephemeral forms of water, clouds, and sky. The surface of the water becomes a constantly moving mosaic of patches of light and color. The luminous summer sky and palpable, humid air of Venice consume the stone churches and palaces, blurring their contours and melting their facades. Corot's *View of Venice* represents a triumph of atmosphere, both visually and metaphorically, as the quiet, lyrical mood of the city encouraged the artist's evocation of the elusive poetry of nature.

123

JEAN BAPTISTE CAMILLE COROT

The Bridge at Mantes

Signed: *Corot*
1868–70
Oil on canvas
46 x 60 cm. (18⅛ x 23⅝ in.)
Inventory no. 443

Corot visited the town of Mantes numerous times from 1845 until his death thirty years later, and represented the bridge in several canvases painted during the 1860s. His predilection for this river scene was surely influenced by his early experience in Venice (see page 123) and by the works of his compatriot Boudin. Moreover, in 1868 Corot visited Daubigny and was encouraged by their mutual interest in *plein-air* painting. Although he sometimes completed his works in the studio, he began his landscapes on the spot, and preserved in the finished painting a sense of the immediacy of vision.

Human beings and structures made by man are included in Corot's scene, an assertion of his conception of nature as man's harmonious environment. Yet human action is subsidiary to the representation of the landscape itself, a view of the irregular masses of buildings and trees against the sky. Silvery light suffuses the atmosphere and unites the composition. In the foreground, the reflections of the river are represented as unbroken and shifting patches of light and color. The water becomes a luminous tapestry emphasizing the surface of the composition. Architectonic forms, the bridge and other structures, are modelled with broad parallel strokes, and their solid shapes are interrupted by planar areas of light and shade. The mood of Corot's scene is evocative and subdued, perhaps even somewhat sad, expressively colored by his overall silver-grey tonality.

125

JEAN BAPTISTE CAMILLE COROT

A Road at Ville-d'Avray

Signed and dated: *Corot, 1874*
Oil on canvas
65 x 50.5 cm. (25⅝ x 19⅞ in.)
Inventory no. 185

Corot frequently worked at Ville-d'Avray throughout his career; his father had bought a house there in 1817, and this view of the road at Ville-d'Avray is signed and dated 1874, one year before the master's death.

The irregular trapezoidal section of the sky is counterbalanced below by the masses of trees and by the road. The road, the wall at the left, and the vegetation at the right plunge diagonally into the distance, where further recession is stopped by the treetops moving across the surface and returning attention to the foreground. Patterns of light and dark also emphasize the surface, forming abstract designs rather than suggesting volumes in space. The bright sunlight casts very strong shadows parallel to the picture plane, and in the background the road's movement into the distance is halted by horizontal bands of shadow. Thus Corot rejects the traditional emphasis on pictorial depth in order to assert the surface of the image—a primary concern of modern art.

People and a dog populate the scene, their profile positions further emphasizing the surface. Corot does not conceive the presence of these figures in any narrative or dramatic way. Like the wall and the road, the figures suggest in a general way man's constructive co-existence with nature. Each element in the scene—human beings, the dirt road, the stone wall, the trees, the sky—is represented with sketchy dashes of color and all are interwoven with Corot's silvery tonality, a unifying atmospheric haze infused with brilliant sunlight. Indeed, this sunlight was Corot's stated theme. In a conversation in 1870 Corot explained the purpose of his art: "It is so good to see the sun . . . I adore its light and have done everything to translate it and to impress others with it as I myself have been impressed."

COROT. 1874.

127

HENRI FANTIN-LATOUR

b. Grenoble, 1836
d. Buré, 1904

Still Life

Signed and dated: *Fantin, 1866*
Oil on canvas
60 x 73 cm. (23⅝ x 28¾ in.)
Inventory no. 67

Although a friend of the Impressionists, especially Manet and Degas, Fantin-Latour preferred a more finished, precise style of painting. In his still lifes he represented flowers and fruits which he arranged carefully and observed objectively. Comparison with Manet's roughly contemporary *Boy with Cherries* or with Monet's rare *Still Life* (pages 133 and 145) shows Fantin-Latour's style to be meticulous and formal, in the older still-life tradition of Chardin. To be sure, Fantin-Latour was interested in the play of light through the crystal vase and water, or the peach's colored reflections on the knife blade, but he did not allow color and light to dominate his sense of solid form. For Fantin-Latour, unlike the Impressionists, color and light are attributes of form, never having their own independent *raison d'être.*

The composition is typical of Fantin-Latour's still-life paintings. The table is set asymmetrically and at a diagonal, and tilted forward somewhat, the better to display the flowers and fruit to the viewer. The background is a monochromatic dark tone, offering no distraction from the richly colored and textured objects on the table. These are Fantin-Latour's protagonists: a white bowl of peaches and figs, a plate of strawberries, a round crystal vase of flowers, two more peaches, one of them cut open, a fruit knife nearby, cherries, and a leafy branch with berries. The knife and branch overlap the edge of the table, seeming to protrude into the viewer's space. And yet the spectator's presence is neither assumed nor invited—only his attention is requested. Artfully and artificially arranged, the flowers and fruit are "posed" in the studio, and do not suggest any human presence. In this sense, Fantin-Latour's *Still Life* is "art for art's sake."

129

EUGENE BOUDIN

b. Honfleur, 1824
d. Deauville, 1898

The Port of Trouville-Deauville

Signed and dated: *E. Boudin, 97*
Oil on panel
31 x 40 cm. (12 1/4 x 15 3/4 in.)
Inventory no. 2282

Boudin was strongly influenced by the color and atmospheric effects of Corot's and Daubigny's art, and early in his career had been particularly encouraged by Millet. In turn, it was Boudin who first led young Claude Monet to an understanding and love of nature, as Monet himself later acknowledged. In his art, Boudin was concerned above all with the aerial qualities of changing weather in a landscape or seascape scene. These scenes were painted directly on the spot, *en plein air*, so as to preserve the fleeting freshness of direct observation. Boudin especially favored water as a motif, and chose compositions such as the *The Port of Trouville-Deauville* because they allowed him to focus upon air and sea. The sky occupies over half the canvas, and the water dominates below, only briefly interrupted by the solid forms of ships, sand, and jetty. Boudin emphasizes air and water precisely because they are the fields on which he can observe light and atmosphere. The scene is enveloped in moist sea air and bathed with a silvery light. Although Boudin does not banish human presence altogether, nonetheless he subjugates man's role and views people in a completely unemotional way, as mere dabs of color against the sky on the left. He evokes and makes permanent the ephemeral scene of shifting light and atmosphere in several ways. The composition itself is asymmetrical, a format influenced by the apparently random scenes of contemporary photography. Boudin alternates areas of light and dark, with light dominating, and applies paint with dashes of the brush. The liveliness of his brushstrokes preserves the creative energy of his simultaneous observation and painting of the scene. He invites the viewer to share his visual and artistic experience with the rapid rhythm and informality of his strokes, handling the paint in a way previously used by artists only for sketching and not for finished works.

EDOUARD MANET

b. Paris, 1832
d. Paris, 1883

Boy with Cherries

Signed: *ed. Manet*
1858
Oil on canvas
65.5 x 54.5 cm. (25 3/4 x 21 1/2 in.)
Inventory no. 395

Manet's *Boy with Cherries* is one of his earliest works, done in his studio in the rue de la Victoire, where the boy Alexandre, who posed for this painting, worked cleaning brushes.

In many ways the composition is traditional, deriving from the formulas of Renaissance portraiture representing figures seen half-length in the foreground of a limited picture space (such as Ghirlandaio's *Portrait*, page 57). Like various Renaissance masters, Manet painted a stone parapet or ledge in the immediate foreground, a form that serves several purposes. Weathered and cracked, it suggests the inexorable passage of time, but it also carries the master's signature inscribed on the surface ("ed. Manet"). This is the artist's assertion that he can evade time, can fix forever ephemeral existence and a transient moment in which cherries fall off a ledge and a bright-eyed boy looks up to grin at the spectator. The parapet ledge, parallel to the picture surface, is also a barrier between the pictorial space and the actual space of the viewer. Yet precisely because the ledge abuts the picture plane, it asserts the immediate proximity of the boy. And when Alexandre's arm and the fruit overhang the parapet, they metaphorically enter the viewer's world.

The influence of Japanese prints, so important to all the Impressionists, is seen here in Manet's strong, decorative contours, especially the asymmetrical outline of the boy's figure against the background. The simple blocks of strong color in Japanese prints inspired the bright red form of the boy's hat. The cherries are a different shade of red, heightened by juxtaposition to the complimentary green of the leaves. Contrasts of light and shade are sudden, stressing surface design rather than three-dimensional space or volume. Manet's rejection of pictorial depth, which had been the great conquest of the Renaissance, and his concomitant emphasis on the surface are the hallmarks of modernity. For all his eclectic borrowings, the young Manet was already highly original, a completely modern master—bold, unsentimental, and forthright in conception and in mood.

133

EDOUARD MANET

Boy Blowing Bubbles

Signed: *Manet*
1867–68
Oil on canvas
100.5 x 81.4 cm. (39 1/2 x 33 1/4 in.)
Inventory no. 2361

Manet's stepson posed for *Boy Blowing Bubbles* in late 1867 or early 1868, and the artist repeated the composition in an engraving in 1869. The theme was suggested by Jean-Baptiste Chardin's *Soap Bubbles* (now in the National Gallery of Washington), while the brisk handling of paint and the neutral tones of the palette are reminiscent of Frans Hals. Black, white, and earth tones dominate, with subtle touches of red in the flesh. As in the early *Boy with Cherries* on the previous page, here too a weathered parapet separates spectator from subject. Here, however, the boy blowing bubbles does not move into the viewer's space or even acknowledge the viewer's existence, but remains completely absorbed in his own activity. His figure is conceived as a strong pattern of light tones dramatically contrasted with the dark ground. He has just produced a perfect soap bubble, which is a *tour de force* of illusionistic painting. Glistening and moist against the background, evanescent and transparent, the bubble is a perfect sphere, just formed and the very image of the ephemeral.

Manet no longer uses light and shadow in the traditional way, with gradual transitions that model forms in space. Rather, abrupt and arbitrary juxtapositions of light and dark emphasize bold surface patterns in the boy's hair, ear, face, and hands. The shadow of the bowl falls on the boy's jacket and merges with the surrounding dark ground. Shadows adhere to the edges of things—to the ridges of folds in the collar and sleeves, to the sides and tips of the boy's fingers. Manet's composition is not a sentimental, anecdotal representation of a child's amusement, but rather a powerful, abstract drama of light and dark, surface and pattern.

135

EDGAR DEGAS

b. Paris, 1834
d. Paris, 1917

Self-Portrait

Ca. 1862
Oil on canvas
92.1 x 69 cm. (36 1/4 x 27 1/8 in.)
Inventory no. 2307

Degas's *Self-Portrait* is almost identical with a photograph of the artist in 1862, now in the Cabinet des Estampes in the Bibliothèque Nationale, Paris. Degas shared with his Impressionist colleague Manet a preference for depictions of contemporary figures represented indoors, and an historical interest in traditional compositional formulas. Like numerous sixteenth-century portraits, Degas's *Self-Portrait* shows the artist three-quarter length and standing at an angle to the picture plane, turning to look toward the spectator. The setting is an interior, but with a window open to reveal landscape and sky, as in many Renaissance paintings. Indeed, the Renaissance device of a window bringing the out-of-doors to an interior is Degas's only allusion to the common Impressionist theme of landscape.

Although these are traditional, even *retardataire* elements in portraiture, Degas's presentation of himself is completely modern. Pose, gesture, and facial expression all convey the same sense of cosmopolitan sophistication. His left hand rests in his trouser pocket; his right casually holds gloves between the fingers, while he tips his hat, saluting the spectator. Originally the artist had drawn the hat close to his face and body, as the painted outline indicates. By moving the hat more to the right, he gave greater prominence to the head and allowed the figure to dominate the picture space more completely. Degas established a relationship between himself and the viewer that is immediate and forceful, and commands our attention by his seemingly spontaneous response to us.

137

EDGAR DEGAS

Portrait of a Painter in His Studio

Signed: *Degas*
1878–79
Oil on canvas
40 x 28 cm. (15¾ x 11 in.)
Inventory no. 420

Although frequently assumed to represent Cézanne, Degas's *Portrait of a Painter* has been more convincingly identified as the Impressionist Henri Michel-Lévy. Degas listed the portrait as the property of a "Mr. H. M.-L." in the catalogue of the 1879 Impressionist show, although the work was not in fact exhibited at that time. Moreover, the painting within the *Portrait*, at the left, is Michel-Lévy's *The Regattas*, which was included in that 1879 show.

The composition is strikingly asymmetrical, with forms cropped by the edges of the picture, in the manner of Japanese prints. Indeed, no form within the painter's studio is complete: the unfinished works, the paint box and palette, the mannequin, even the painter himself—all are interrupted by the picture edges or by each other. This cropping establishes a feeling of malaise, heightened by the jarring diagonals of the room and the shapes of the paintings and paint box, which come to no easy resolution but war with each other, pulling in different directions. The placement of the figures, both human and inanimate, also creates a dramatic tension. Michel-Lévy is markedly off-center in the picture space, leaning against one of his unfinished canvases and looking through hooded eyes at the spectator. The mannequin, almost a mirror of herself in Michel-Lévy's painting at the left, turns her back on the artist. At the same time, her graceless, limp position implies pathetically that she has been discarded or rejected. Degas thus represents the painful loneliness imposed by creativity—the artist's only companions are his own painted beings and a lifeless doll, and he is alienated even from them. Nor do the painter's stance and suspicious gaze invite metaphoric intimacy with the spectator. And, most disturbing in this context, the artist's hands are in his pockets. Earlier and contemporary portraits and self-portraits of artists often show painters holding their brushes, but Michel-Lévy's brushes and palette are not in use: he is estranged even from his own creativity. The artist's mute, lonely enclosure in his studio is all the more bitter in juxtaposition with his own Impressionist works of gregarious ladies and gentlemen in sunny landscape settings.

degas

139

MARY CASSATT

b. Pittsburgh, 1845
d. Mesnil-Beaufresne, France, 1927

The Stocking

Signed: *Mary Cassatt*
Ca. 1891
Pastel
78 x 57 cm. (30 3/4 x 22 1/2 in.)
Inventory no. 39

A mother with her child was Mary Cassatt's favorite theme—not the Madonna and Christ Child of earlier generations, however, but common people in ordinary situations. Their moods and movements are completely natural and guileless. Such artlessness and truth to life are typical of the characters in scenes by Cassatt's colleagues, the French Impressionists. In fact, Cassatt was the only American member of that group, having exhibited with the Impressionists since 1877, at the invitation of Edgar Degas. Cassatt's unidealized representations were particularly influenced by Degas's sometimes brutal honesty. She chose to depict mundane, often awkward actions previously ignored by artists, such as a woman pulling on a baby's stocking. Around 1890, Cassatt made two pencil drawings of that subject (now in a private collection in Paris and in the Rhode Island School of Design), and these sheets may be understood as preparatory studies for the Gulbenkian pastel. In the drawings, however, the baby is nude and in three-quarter profile, while his mother is in full profile. In the pastel, Cassatt has achieved an even more lifelike sense of action and tenderness of mood. The baby turns to his left and extends his arm, his plump hand open as though grasping for someone or something out of reach. His mother looks down at his foot to pull on the stocking and holds her son firmly on her lap between her hands. The composition is boldly asymmetrical, reflecting an appreciation for Japanese prints shared by all the Impressionists. The muted colors and the luminosity of Cassatt's work also reveal the influence of Manet.

Cassatt's conception is at once powerful in composition and gentle in tone. The mother's loving tranquility is counterbalanced by the child's lively movement; her pose, closed protectively over and around her child, is juxtaposed with his open posture, as he turns and reaches outward, though not beyond the real and symbolic boundaries of his mother's arms.

140

141

PIERRE AUGUSTE RENOIR

b. Limoges, 1841
d. Cagnes, 1919

Portrait of Madame Claude Monet

1872
Oil on canvas
53 x 71.7 cm. (20 7/8 x 28 1/4 in.)
Inventory no. 2301

Renoir painted the wife of his friend Claude Monet while visiting them at their house in Argenteuil in 1872. The portrait remained in the family's possession until Michel Monet sold it to Paul Rosenberg, who sold it to Gulbenkian.

Of all the Impressionists, Renoir was by far the most joyous and the most congenial in his art, in a sense the heir of Boucher and Fragonard. While Monet generally excluded human beings from his canvases, Renoir's are peopled with gregarious and happy individuals. Usually Renoir represented figures out of doors, but this *Portrait of Madame Claude Monet* shows Camille at home, reclining on a sofa and reading a newspaper, *Le Figaro*. Nevertheless, Renoir painted Camille in her room with the same atmospheric effects that characterize his *plein-air* compositions. Lines do not exist in Renoir's portrait: forms are suggested by delicate, fluid strokes of color, permeated by a diffused light and atmosphere. Sometimes Renoir's free brushstrokes establish only areas of color and light, and are liberated from the traditional role of creating forms. For example, the drapery of Camille's gown does not model or define her figure, but is self-justified as color mottled with light. Touches of bright red on her sleeve and on a bowl next to her hand cannot be read as forms or patterns. The red is freed from any specific representational function, and is included as patches of pure vivid color. Even the bold typeface of the newspaper's title dissolves in Renoir's atmosphere, and is illegible. Only the great familiarity of the publication allows the viewer to identify it by guessing, rather than by reading the letters.

Renoir almost negates spaces in the traditional pictorial sense. Various bluish-white areas—the sofa, pillows, wall, stockings, even the newspaper—all seem to meld and blend as though liquid. His effervescent style, his sketchy, free, and seemingly haphazard handling of paint communicate the master's *joie de vivre* and intoxicate the viewer with the sensual pleasure of seeing.

143

CLAUDE MONET

b. Paris, 1840
d. Giverny, 1926

Still Life

Signed: *Claude Monet*
Ca. 1876
Oil on canvas
53 x 73 cm. (20 7/8 x 28 3/4 in.)
Inventory no. 450

This *Still Life* is an unusual work by the great Impressionist Monet, who was dedicated to open-air landscape painting, which meant for him the careful observation of changing effects of weather. But Monet has brought to this uncustomary subject the technical verve and energy that characterize his out-of-doors landscapes. Brushstrokes are dense daubs of color, sometimes interwoven, sometimes with a clear juxtaposition of different hues. Monet has varied his handling of pigment to represent the different textures of the fruits and objects in the painting. He suggests the hard, light-reflecting surface of the china plate, the soft fuzziness of the peaches, the smooth, shiny grapes, the rough shell of the melon next to its moist flesh. All the fruit here is ripe and explicitly ready to eat, so that although no human being is represented, yet a human presence is felt, or invited.

Monet has arranged his composition with great care, and the *Still Life* naturally appears more consciously structured than his landscapes. He has emphasized tones of blue and orange, unifying the scene chromatically with these complementary colors. The formal theme, so to speak, is the circle or sphere. A seemingly haphazard pyramid of globular peaches is placed off-center in front of a round blue and white china plate. Here Monet sets actual nature—the peaches—against fictive nature—the china plate painted with leaves and flowers. To the right, the grapes, smaller spheres, lie in front of the melon, sliced for serving. Dark shadows alternate with bright highlights, especially the plate's shadow against the melon skin, and the interior of the melon casting shadows upon itself. The succulent fruit, particularly the melon, is endowed with an expressive force and with powerful sensuous connotations. In this painting Monet seems to evoke the compositions and the sensuality of Cézanne's still lifes.

145

CLAUDE MONET

The Breakup of the Ice

Signed and dated: *Claude Monet, 80*
1880
Oil on canvas
68 x 90 cm. (26 3/4 x 35 1/2 in.)
Inventory no. 451

Painted on the Seine near Vétheuil, *The Breakup of the Ice* is perhaps the greatest of a series of compositions of ice on the river on which Monet worked in 1880 and 1881. Camille, his first wife, had died in 1879, and the frozen scene seems permeated with feelings of desolation.

The composition is divided almost equally between the icy river and the cloudy sky, with barely an indication of solid land. The meagre trees at the right have been all but overpowered by the floods and ice— they seem to shiver and bend in the cold. A few houses in the central background appear pathetic and abandoned. Ice itself is the protagonist here, its slabs and chunks suggested by Monet's dashes of color, the strokes in contrast to the more smoothly painted water. At the same time, Monet also evokes the pace and movement of the breaking ice, thereby indicating the transience of this moment: his constant concern in his landscape painting was the depiction of ephemeral atmospheric effects. This winter scene is unified and dominated by a shroud of damp, frigid air.

Monet represented depth in landscape in several ways. In the traditional manner of European painting, he indicates the far distance with hazier color and handling than in the foreground. In an entirely original way, he conveys the depth of the river with the varied texture, direction and thickness of his brushstrokes. The surface is almost woven like a fabric, or constructed like a mosaic, with dabs of color and light replacing the tesserae. Monet's composition and handling— though not the melancholic mood and cold palette—foreshadow his late Water Lily series.

147

AUGUSTE RODIN

b. Paris, 1840
d. Meudon, 1917

Jean d'Aire, Burgher of Calais

Signed: *A. Rodin*
1884–95
Bronze
207 cm. high (81 ½ in.)
Inventory no. 567

In 1884, the city of Calais commissioned the sculptor Auguste Rodin to represent a group commemorating six heroic citizens of the distant past as an exemplar of civic virtue for the present. The six leading citizens of Calais had offered themselves to Edward III of England that he might lift the siege of their city in 1346–47. Wearing sackcloth and rope halters, the Burghers believed that they were going to certain death—although in fact they were later spared by King Edward for their heroism. The Gulbenkian bronze is a cast of the first citizen on the right in the group, Jean d' Aire, who holds before him the keys of the citadel of Calais. The sculpture is signed by the artist and was acquired by Gulbenkian from Rodin himself.

In order that the Burghers' exemplary patriotism should inspire the modern-day citizens of Calais, Rodin set the figures on a low base, close to the ground and hence to the spectator, rather than on a high pedestal, which had been traditional for public monuments. The proximity of the sculpture to the viewer is emphasized by the tactile quality of the bronze, deeply modelled to produce strong variations of light and shade; these patterns of light and dark become the abstract expressions of the Burgher's state of mind. "To model shadows," Rodin explained, "is to create thoughts." The sculptor intended that the Burghers appeal to the viewer's sense of touch, and that in touching the figures the spectators would also enhance the patina of the bronze. Thus Rodin meant to establish both the actual presence of the Burghers in the viewer's world, and the literal, physical interaction of the viewer with them. This physical closeness heightens the emotional impact of the work. Rodin's theme is the same throughout the group, albeit interpreted differently according to the particular character of each individual figure: the innate, unconquerable nobility of the common man.

However, while involving the spectator emotionally with their inspiring patriotism and their spiritual strength, the Burghers are nonetheless tragically isolated. Each is alone as he confronts death. No one can accompany him in death, not even another of his compatriots. Thus the sculpture mingles pathos with nobility.

148

EDWARD BURNE-JONES

b. Birmingham, 1833
d. London, 1898

The Mirror of Venus

Signed and dated: *E. Burne-Jones,
    1875*
Oil on canvas
120 x 200 cm. (47 1/4 x 78 3/4 in.)
Inventory no. 273

Edward Burne-Jones was associated with the Pre-Raphaelite movement in England, and especially with Dante Gabriel Rossetti. These artists aimed to represent reality with what their champion John Ruskin called "truth to nature." Their truth was not the optical, impartial accuracy of the French Impressionists, but was based on personal experience and characterized by a decorative treatment of line, color, and composition.

For Burne-Jones, reality in painting existed in the precise observation of detail. Thus, in *The Mirror of Venus*, he has represented everything with crystalline clarity, emphasizing the minute details of forms near and far—individual, nervous folds of drapery, the distinct petals of flowers, the veins of water lily pads, the surface variations of the rocky terrain. Burne-Jones's pond is indeed glassy, literally a mirror, as the title claims. His precise, smooth brushstrokes and the highly finished quality of his work are strikingly different from the sketchy style of contemporary Impressionist painting, such as Boudin's *View of Trouville* (page 131). Yet each artist intended that his image be faithful to nature's reality.

Again, unlike his French contemporaries, Burne-Jones favored figure painting over landscape, and subjects drawn from the distant past over those of the present. The Elgin Marbles (the Parthenon sculptures in the British Museum) moved him deeply, and in *The Mirror of Venus* both the frieze-like composition and the classical subject are inspired by ancient Greece. His slender classical maidens, fragile and slightly sad, admire their reflections in a mirror of water, each different from the next in posture, facial expression, and the color of her gown. Burne-Jones intended his Romantic themes to combat the grey dreariness of modern industrial life. He achieved this aim with the brightness and variety of his colors, his richly decorative vision, and his creation of a fantastic, idealized past.

RENE LALIQUE

b. Aÿ, Marne, 1860
d. Paris, 1945

Cock Diadem

Ca. 1898
Gold and enamel with amethyst
9 x 15 cm. (3½ x 5⅞ in.)
Inventory no. 1208

It was the fashion in the Second Empire, during the reign of Louis-Philippe, only to wear jewelry bearing precious stones. After the opening of the diamond mines in South Africa in 1870, the purity, brilliance, and size of the stones in a brooch or necklace became most important, while the role of the goldsmith was reduced. The purpose of jewelry was solely to satisfy vanity.

The Art Nouveau movement, which sprang into being around 1880 and lasted into the 1910s, rejected such thinking. It aimed to make objects of decoration and art harmonize with ideals of feminine beauty, and drew its inspiration from nature and fantasy. Art Nouveau jewelry placed great emphasis on the skills of the craftsman, and its own beauty arose from the exotic designs used, not from the preciosity of the materials.

The cock diadem shown here exemplifies Lalique's concern to make a piece of jewelry a work of art in its own right. It was designed to decorate and adorn, rather than to be a display of wealth. The delicate filigree gold and enamel work are truly remarkable. The large stone in the bird's beak is an amethyst, although it originally held a diamond.

152

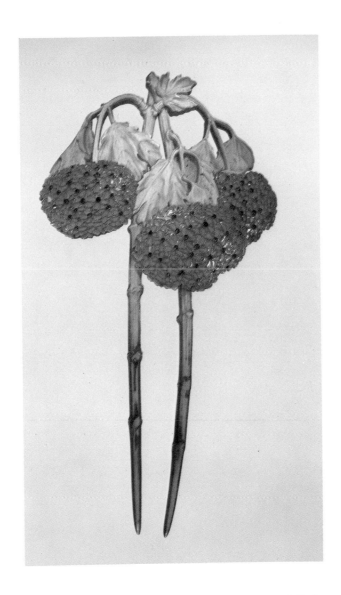

RENE LALIQUE

Hydrangea Hair Comb

Ca. 1903–04
Gold, enamel, and diamonds on horn
16 x 8 cm. (6 ¼ x 3 ⅛ in.)
Inventory no. 1210

The artistry and design of Lalique's jewelry supplanted the heavy, Victorian precious-stone pieces that had been in vogue. He often used semi-precious stones, enamel, and even carved glass—colored, iridescent, or opaque. He was the first jeweller to use carved horn for the hair combs worn by women in the elaborate hairstyles of the time.

This comb in the form of a spray of hydrangea blossoms illustrates Lalique's unusual use of horn; it is embellished with enamel and gold and enhanced by a scattering of diamonds, meant to suggest dew on the flowers. This use of materials to simulate nature is typical of Art Nouveau style, which often shows a touch of wit. The pale, delicate colors and languid, drooping flowers also reflect the Art Nouveau sense of beauty as a frail, graceful, ephemeral thing.

153

RENE LALIQUE

Dragonfly Corsage Ornament

Signed: *Lalique*
Ca. 1898
Enamelled gold with chrysoprase
23 x 26.6 cm. (9 x 10 1/2 in.)
Inventory no. 1197

Lalique infused his art with a spirit, an imagination, a taste that became paradigms of the jeweller's craft. For him, nature was the inspiration for an infinite number of motifs. He often linked the female figure with nature in an exotic guise: a swan, a lotus flower, a dragonfly. The famous corsage ornament pictured here is in the form of a dragonfly-woman whose nude torso rises out of the gaping jaws of a lizard with enormous clawed feet. Gulbenkian lent this particular piece to Sarah Bernhardt, who was one of Lalique's patrons.

Like the use of enamels and other inexpensive materials, the image of a monstrous creature in a piece of jewelry was an innovation of the artist. Here the influence of Japanese art, which was pervasive in Art Nouveau, may be seen. Insects and small creatures are common in the art of Japan (see page 205), and were transformed in the art of *fin-de-siècle* Paris into objects as beautiful and exotic as they are grotesque.

RENE LALIQUE

Serpents' Knot Corsage Ornament

Signed: *Lalique*
Ca. 1898
Enamelled silver gilt
20.8 x 14.3 cm. (8 1/4 x 5 5/8 in.)
Inventory no. 1216

The artist has used this serpent pin as a showpiece to display his mastery of technique, creating a theme that reflects his love of the eccentric, the monstrous, the fantastic—be it chimera, fabulous animal, or serpent. Lalique gave form to the images of his imagination in pendants, bracelets, combs, and hairpins, rich with colors, patterns, and gems, wrought with astonishing craftsmanship.

Art Nouveau arose out of a mingling of influences. Among these were a taste for the medieval—visible in the deep colors, cloisonné, and mimicry of stained glass in jewelry and other decorative arts—and an appreciation of the sinuous lines of Japanese art. It is interesting, therefore, to compare this bibelot with the Japanese box pictured on page 201, which also has a snake decoration.

RENE LALIQUE

Mask Brooch

Signed: *Lalique*
Ca. 1900
Crystal and silver with baroque pearl
9.8 x 5.2 cm. (3 7/8 x 2 1/16 in.)
Inventory no. 1141

156

Lalique's art has a delicacy and mood that pay homage to the Parisian women of his time. As with the piece illustrated here, the female face was often used, her hair flowing and curling, undulating into ribbons, leaves, or flowers. Intertwining creepers, vines, and blossoms (cornflowers in the case of this unusual brooch) were frequently used by Art Nouveau artists: this face is reminiscent of the women in Alphonse Mucha's famous posters. Lalique's inclusion of a baroque pearl is a major departure from tradition. For two hundred years pearls of imperfect shape had been considered ugly and cheap, but he used them often, echoing the taste of the early Renaissance so much admired at the turn of the century.

RENE LALIQUE

Plaque from a Dog-collar

Signed: *Lalique*
Ca. 1899–1900
Chrysoprase, gold, and enamel
5 x 8.6 cm. (2 x 3⅜ in.)
Inventory no. 1133

Like the brooch on the facing page, this plaque (meant to be worn at a woman's throat) celebrates feminine beauty, making it visually synonymous with the beauty of flora. The flowers here are lotuses, which frame the elegant profile in a manner at once exotic and archaic. The face itself is modelled on a classical facial type, emphasized by the ribbon bound across the brows in the style of Greek or Roman sculpture. The silhouette thus embodies a feminine ideal.

157

The
Near and
Middle Eastern
Collection

PERSIAN (IRAN), NISHAPUR OR KASHAN

Bottle

Twelfth or thirteenth century
Alkaline glazed ceramic
30 cm. high (11 3/4 in.)
Inventory no. 936

This glazed earthenware bottle was perhaps intended as a receptacle for wine at banquets or celebrations. In Iran, turquoise blue was considered emblematic of success and good fortune. A festive mood is also suggested by the vessel's relief decoration, which depicts a stylized human face in alternation with high-footed ewers. In Persian poetry it was customary to compare beautiful women with the full moon luminous in the night sky. The exaggerated rotundity of the faces on this bottle was perhaps intended to evoke this metaphor in the spectator's mind. Ewers of the type depicted on this bottle were used in eastern Iran during the eleventh and twelfth centuries, which suggests that this bottle was also made in that region. Nishapur was one of the most important ceramic producing centers of eastern Iran and kilns excavated there have yielded numerous molds for decorating ceramics. Some of them have produced vessels with a series of faces in relief around their circumference. Another popular design was ribs or flutes resembling those on this bottle. Thus elements in the decoration of this bottle link it with vessels produced in Nishapur. It is known, however, that molded vessels were also made in central Iran at Kashan, for a bowl bearing the signature of a potter from that city has been found. In Kashan, bottles of this general shape were often decorated with lustre painting. It is probable, therefore, that bottles resembling this one were also made at Kashan. Several other bottles with relief decoration are preserved in museum collections, but normally the molded design shows animals against a foliage background.

160

P. S.

PERSIAN (IRAN), KASHAN

Bowl

Twelfth/thirteenth centuries
Tin glazed ceramic; under- and
  overglaze painted
8 cm. high, 18 cm. in diameter
  (3 1/8 x 7 1/8 in.)
Inventory no. 935

Produced in central Iran during the late twelfth or early thirteenth century, this bowl exemplifies the qualities most admired by Iranian connoisseurs. Both its eight-lobed shape and white-glazed surface have a Far Eastern inspiration, while its pictorial and calligraphic embellishment follow Near Eastern traditions. Chinese ceramics are known to have reached the Near East as early as the eighth century. Particularly popular were porcelain bowls, admired for their delicate shapes and nearly translucent walls. During the tenth and eleventh centuries, lobed bowls must have been much in demand because fragments of Chinese vessels in such shapes have been excavated in Iran, Iraq, and Egypt. In its shape, therefore, this bowl imitates a Chinese type popular in the Near East, but its white-glazed surface is embellished with painting in a Near Eastern technique. By placing some pigments under the glaze and others over it, Iranian potters were able to use a wide range of colors. Particularly difficult was the firing of overglaze pigments, for which a special kiln was used. In Iran, ceramics of this type appear to have been made principally in the city of Kashan.

The theme depicted on this bowl is also of Near Eastern inspiration. Painted on the bowl's interior is a youth seated on a high-backed throne, encircled by four riders and four pairs of birds flanking medallions. On the exterior an inscription offers wishes of longevity and power to the vessel's owner. The interior decoration of a prince surrounded by his entourage may be intended as an idealized portrait of the owner addressed in the exterior inscriptions. During the twelfth and thirteenth centuries, Iran was ruled by a number of military figures, each with their own supporters, and this bowl provides a benign abbreviated reference to their way of life. Two of the riders carry polo sticks, so the potter may have wished to depict a polo game played in the presence of a prince.

162

P. S.

163

PERSIAN (IRAN), KASHAN

Prayer Niche

Thirteenth/fourteenth centuries
Molded ceramic; lustre and
  underglaze painted
63 x 47 cm. (24 3/4 x 18 1/2 in.)
Inventory no. 1567

During the thirteenth and early fourteenth centuries, potters in the Iranian city of Kashan were renowned for their skill in producing ceramics for architectural use. This plaque once belonged to the wall revetments of a religious building, where it served to designate the direction of Mecca toward which all Muslims must pray. Formed in a mold, key elements in the design were highlighted with underglaze blue. After the piece had been fired, the background was painted with metallic oxides which became lustrous after a supplementary firing in a reducing kiln. The skills needed to produce and decorate such plaques were handed down from generation to generation among the potters of Kashan, and tiles from their workshops adorned many important religious and secular buildings. Despite the general decline in Iran after the Mongol conquests of the thirteenth century, the potters of Kashan continued to be active and tiles from their workshops decorated many of the buildings erected by the new rulers. In this instance, the Koranic inscriptions that cover much of its surface suggest it was made for a tomb. It had been reported that it comes from the tomb of one of the Mongols who had converted to Islam, Muhammad Uljaitu, who was buried in an impressive tomb constructed in the city of Sultaniyyah, which he himself had founded. Here, carefully chosen verses from three sections of the Koran are used. The boldly executed text of the outer frame is Sura 110, which would be particularly appropriate for a convert to Islam:

> When comes the help of God, and victory,
> and thou seest men entering God's religion in throngs,
> then proclaim the praise of thy Lord, and seek his forgiveness,
> for He turns again unto men.

The inner arch is inscribed with the opening invocation of the Koran, often used as a prayer, and within the arch is Sura 41:30 which speaks of the rewards awaiting the faithful:

> Those who have said, "Our Lord is God,"
> then have gone straight, upon them the
> angels descend, saying "Fear not,
> neither sorrow, rejoice in Paradise
> that you were promised."

These words are placed around a lamp, a frequent symbol of divine illumination in Islam (see page 183).

164

P. S.

165

CENTRAL ASIAN, SAMARQAND

Jug

1417–49
Jade
14.5 cm. high (5 3/4 in.)
Inventory no. 328

Made of white jade, this jug belonged to three Islamic rulers in turn. The names and titles of its original owner, Ulugh Beg, are carved around the vessel's neck:

> The Great Sultan, Supporter of the World and the Faith,
> Ulugh Beg Gurkan, May His Realm and Reign endure.

More inconspicuous is the inscription of Jihangir, the Mughal emperor, incised on the rim, and that of his son Shah Jihan, placed below the handle. Ulugh Beg, a grandson of Timur, lived most of his life in Samarqand and this jug was probably carved there. Born in 1394, he was installed as ruler of Samarqand in 1409 and ruled there until his death in 1449. The great conqueror Timur dreamed of recreating the Mongol Empire that once had stretched from Anatolia to China, and his descendants also showed enthusiasm for Mongol traditions. Ulugh Beg had two wives descended from the Mongols who continued to rule the region now occupied by the Kirgiz in the U.S.S.R. and the Sinkiang region of China. These marriages entitled him to use the title *Gurkan*, designating him as son-in-law of a Mongol ruler. He also made periodic raids into areas east of Samarqand, where the Mongols and other nomadic groups lived, a region long famous for its jade. During an expedition in 1425, he acquired two large boulders of jade which he had transported to Samarqand and used to construct a cenotaph over Timur's grave.

In both China and the Near East, jade was credited with magical powers. In the Near East it was believed to react to poison by splitting; thus, a jade cup would safeguard its owner against noxious substances. Ulugh Beg is known to have owned at least two jade cups. One now in the British Museum has a shallow shape and dragon handle deriving from Chinese models. This one imitates the form of metal vessels made in fifteenth-century Iran, but its handle probably also echoes Chinese styles. As descendants of Timur, the Mughal emperors of India were anxious to perpetuate Timurid traditions. In his memoirs Jihangir describes receiving a cup very similar to this one as a gift from one of his courtiers. It

> had been made in the reign of Mirza Ulugh Beg Gurgan, in
> the honoured name of that prince. It was a very delicate
> rarity and of a beautiful shape. Its stone was exceedingly
> white and pure. Around the neck they had carved the name of
> the auspicious Mirza and the Hijra year in ruq'a characters.
> I ordered them to inscribe my name and the auspicious name of
> Akbar on the edge of the lip of the jar.

Jihangir received this gift in August 1607 and the jug now in Lisbon is inscribed with the date of 1613. Despite this difference and other small variations between the inscriptions mentioned by Jihangir and those on the Lisbon jug, it is possible that the vessel he describes receiving is the one illustrated here.

P. S.

167

PERSIAN (IRAN), SHIRAZ

The Lovesick Beggar

Page from the *Bustan* of Sa'di
1536–37
Tempera on paper
29.5 x 19 cm. (11 5/8 x 7 1/2 in.)
Inventory no. LA 180

Since its completion in 1257, the *Bustan* of Sa'di has had an enduring popularity in the Iranian world. Given the name *Bustan*, which means orchard or garden, the work consists of more than a hundred moralistic stories written in verse and grouped according to their themes. This painting from the section on love shows the plight of a beggar who had fallen in love with a prince after seeing him once and thereafter spent his days before the palace of his beloved hoping to meet him again. In depicting the beggar's passion the painter has shown him in conversation with a white-bearded man in the midst of a polo field. This setting is suggested, although not described, by Sa'di's text, which compares the beggar standing before the palace to a goalpost, and by the verses immediately above the painting:

> "But what," said the other "if you are wounded by his polo-stick?"
> Said he: "Then like the ball, at his feet I will fall!"

Persian poets often used the game of polo as a metaphor for love, but clearly the beggar is ill equipped to participate in such a contest and could only be the recipient of blows from the polo-stick of his beloved. Indeed, Sa'di stresses the manner in which the beggar's all-consuming love for the prince makes him oblivious to discomfort and even pain. The form of love represented by this story, which stressed purification through suffering, was given a quasi-religious interpretation by many Persian poets and religious thinkers. It was often compared to quest of the soul for unity with the Divine Creator. In showing the beggar clad only in a skirt, the painter reminds us of his asceticism.

Beyond the remarks in Sa'di's poem the painter may have drawn on his own experience in selecting the theme of a polo game to symbolize the life of a prince. Polo was a favorite pastime of Iranian rulers and their courtiers both in Sa'di's lifetime and in the sixteenth century when this manuscript was copied (see page 163). Often, polo fields were adjacent to royal residences.

P. S.

PERSIAN (IRAN), TABRIZ

Bookbinding

Ca. 1480
Molded leather over cardboard
20.8 x 11.4 cm. (8 3/16 x 4 1/2 in.)
Inventory no. R.37

Embellished with pictorial decoration and having a verse inscribed on its flap, this binding probably covered a poetic manuscript. On each of its principal sections—front cover, back cover, and flap—a different scene is depicted. Created by the use of large stamps applied to dampened leather, pictorial compositions of this sort were popular in Iran during the fifteenth century and appear on manuscripts produced in Herat, Shiraz, and Tabriz. Frequently, the inner faces of such bindings were decorated with designs cut from leather or paper; here, a medallion composition is used. The theme depicted on this binding's exterior—a princely hunting preserve—was often used on manuscripts of poetry. In this binding the compositions are notable for their anecdotal details. Narrative elements are introduced into each scene, giving the compositions greater psychological unity. On the front cover a youthful archer is shown with his arm raised, having just shot an arrow at a lion which is attacking a small bear. Below, monkeys play in a tree and above a bear hoists a boulder over its head. The antics of bears are also shown on the back cover, where one is chased by a fox and another lunges toward a rabbit, which looks disdainfully in the other direction. Also shown are a gazelle and a deer under a tree. The landscape is framed by ducks flying amidst clouds across the top and swimming in a stream filled with fish along the bottom. On the flap a bird of prey alights on a rabbit while a pair of foxes scurry away from their erstwhile quarry.

These compositions, with their wealth of detail and finely executed elements, must have been designed by an important painter. Very similar scenes are used to decorate a binding made in Tabriz for Yaqub Aq Qoyunlu, who ruled western Iran from 1478 to 1490. Particularly similar to manuscripts made at his court is the style of the princely figure depicted on this binding's front cover. The popularity of scenes showing a royal hunting preserve derives in part from the existence of such parks around the dwellings of princes and in part from a pictorial tradition of Chinese origin. This was probably known in Iran through its use on objects brought there as gifts for local rulers by envoys from the Ming emperors. Combining elements from the Near Eastern princely tradition of the hunt with exotic landscape features of Far Eastern origin, this binding reveals more about the taste of its original owner that about the contents of the book it once covered.

P. S.

PERSIAN (IRAN)

Bookbinding

Sixteenth century
Molded and gilded leather over
   cardboard, with cut-paper inserts
49.6 x 33.2 cm. (19 1/2 x 13 1/8 in.)
Inventory no. R.20

With its rich contrasts of pattern and color, this binding shows the work of Islamic binders at its most lavish. Koranic verses inscribed on both the cover and flap indicate that it once covered a manuscript of the Koran. Customarily, Islamic bindings have two covers and a flap which is folded over the fore-edge of the book and tucked under its front cover. Reproduced here are a back cover and its attached flap. In the first centuries of the Islamic era, Koranic manuscripts were often copied in an impressive and well-proportioned script, but their bindings appear to have been simple, consisting of leather stretched over boards made up of many layers of paper pasted one to another. Gradually, leather covers were given more elaborate decoration with stamped and gilded patterns. During the fifteenth century, two new techniques became popular: the use of large stamps to create pictorial decoration (see previous page) and the creation of patterns in cut leather or paper. Usually stamped patterns were used on the exterior and filigree work on the interior. During the sixteenth century, filigree work was also used on some portions of the binding's outer cover. Here the panels of cut leather, backed by contrasting colors, are inset into the cardboard backing and thus protected by raised leather areas. Molds were used to create the design of arabesques and cloud-bands that covers the central zone of the binding as well as for the panels of the interior border. Pulverized gold suspended in a medium such as fish glue was often painted on sections of a binding. Here it is used to add painted decoration to the flap and to enhance the molded designs. In its general arrangement of medallions and borders, this binding resembles illuminated pages placed at the beginning of manuscripts. Similar designs were also used for carpets (see following page).

The Koranic verses that encircle the central medallion on both cover and flap stress the differing reactions of Muslims and non-Muslims to its text.

> Ours it is to gather it and to recite it.
> So when We recite it, follow thou its recitation.
>
> When thou recitest the Koran, We place between thee and those who do not believe in the world to come a curtain obstructing.

P. S.

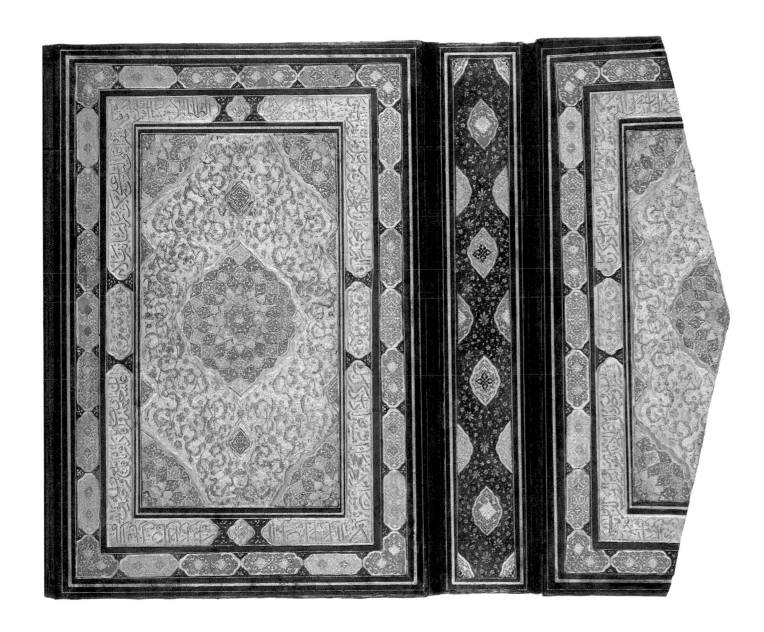

173

PERSIAN (IRAN), KASHAN(?)

Carpet

Sixteenth/seventeenth centuries
Silk
230 x 180 cm. (90 1/2 x 70 7/8 in.)
Inventory no. T.100

In a highly stylized fashion, this carpet evokes the memory of a garden or hunting preserve filled with flowering trees and plants and inhabited by exotic birds and animals. Its general scheme of central and corner medallions, framed by a series of borders, derives from manuscript illumination and bookbinding (see previous page). Being both knotted and woven of silk, it has over six hundred knots per square inch, allowing for the execution of a complex and fluid design. Each zone of the carpet has its own theme. The main field contains pairs of animals in combat. Some, like the lions and gazelles, would have been found in a royal hunting preserve, but others with wings and exotic markings inhabit the realm of the imagination. Brightly plumaged pheasants perch on large blossoms in the main border and small birds flutter among vines in the corner medallions. Most exotic of all is the central medallion, in which pairs of dragons and phoenixes are placed against a dark green ground. Used in China as emblems of the emperor and his consort, the dragon and phoenix also served as emblems of royal power in Iran during the fifteenth and sixteenth centuries.

Both the date and provenance of this carpet have been subjects of debate among scholars of Near Eastern art. It is known that during the seventeenth century silk carpets were produced in the city of Kashan and some would place this carpet among them, but would date it to the sixteenth century. Others have placed it in Isfahan or Kirman, and suggest that it was produced in the early seventeenth century. A connection can be seen between the leaves and blossoms of this carpet's outer border and the borders used on "vase carpets," often associated with Kirman (see page 177). In various sections of this carpet can be seen composite blossoms deriving from Far Eastern representations of the lotus. These richly colored flowers are given a more geometric and angular appearance in the vase carpets, providing another link between the two series of carpets. Whatever its date or provenance this carpet exemplifies the courtly tradition of Persian carpet production.

P. S.

175

PERSIAN (IRAN), KIRMAN(?)

Carpet

Seventeenth century
Wool
434 x 183 cm. (170 7/8 x 72 in.)
Inventory no. T.70

Despite the variety of colors and patterns used in this carpet, its design is highly organized. Two systems of stems, one blue, the other yellow, run the length of the field, dividing it into a series of overlapping pointed oval zones. Large composite blossoms lie along the path of the stems with each system having vertically placed flowers in alternation with those on the diagonal. A third series of stems connects the various smaller blossoms that lie between the larger ones. This arrangement creates a design on three intersecting planes and produces an orderly but complex pattern. Carpets of this type are often described as "vase carpets" because of the small vases that appear at intervals along the central axis of the design. These vases are, however, only incidental elements in a design dominated by composite blossoms arranged along a trellis-like lattice. These blossoms have parallels in architectural decoration of seventeenth-century Isfahan. Similar flowers are found in both tiles and wall paintings. The basic scheme of this design was probably influenced by patterns used in silk brocades of the late sixteenth century. Ultimately, many of the blossoms in this carpet are stylized variants of the lotus, a decorative theme that became popular in Iran after the Mongol conquests of the thirteenth century, when Chinese decorative motifs were introduced into the Near Eastern repertoire.

Special features in the weaving of vase carpets, such as the use of three unequal wefts after every row of knots, connect them to carpets traditionally associated with the city of Kirman in southeastern Iran, and this carpet may have been woven there during the seventeenth century. Later carpets have a simplified version of this lattice scheme and very schematic versions of this design were still used in the Caucasus during the eighteenth and nineteenth centuries. The abstract designs that predominate in vase carpets made them appropriate for use in religious buildings and some are known to have been made for shrines. The patterns were, however, also suitable for domestic use and many must have been placed in the reception rooms of Persian homes.

176

P. S.

177

PERSIAN (IRAN)

Man's Coat

Eighteenth/nineteenth centuries
Silk
104 cm. high (41 in.)
Inventory no. 1382

This man's coat typifies the opulent taste in clothing favored in Indian and Persian court circles. Adapted in basic cut from European garments, coats made of heavy silk brocade were popular in India during the seventeenth century and in Iran during the eighteenth and early nineteenth centuries. Probably intended for winter use, such coats were normally worn with a fur neckpiece or collar. In India these coats were often made of gold brocade decorated with floral sprays and were customarily worn over a full-skirted dress-like garment. The fashion of wearing such coats may have originated at the Mughal court and then spread to other centers. A portrait of the Mughal prince Dara Shikoh, painted around 1650, shows him wearing a coat of this type made of gold cloth decorated with clumps of flowers. By 1680 the style had reached the central Indian kingdom of Golconda, as can be seen from portraits of its ruler, Abul Hassan. Envoys of Indian rulers to the Persian court may have introduced the style to Iran during the seventeenth century, but its greatest popularity there came only during the late eighteenth century and after.

In pattern, the fabrics used for this coat follow Indian precedent and may even be of Indian manufacture. Its cut, however, is typical of early nineteenth-century Persian garments. Fath 'Ali Shah Qajar, who ruled Iran from 1797 to 1834, often wore garments made of gold brocade embellished with clumps of flowers, and he also favored garments fitted tightly at the waist and with sleeves tapered to a point. In paintings, his courtiers are often shown wearing gold-brocaded coats with fur neckpieces, and the popularity of this style may have been due to a vogue for Indian taste at the Qajar court. Persian coats differ from Indian ones in having a more flaring skirt and in the use of buttons on the chest and sleeves. Because of their tight fit, the coats were often buttoned only at the waist and the sleeves worn unbuttoned, with the tips folded back.

178

P. S.

SYRIAN

Beaker

Fourteenth century
Enamelled and gilded glass
33.5 cm. high (13 3/16 in.)
Inventory no. 2378

During the thirteenth and fourteenth centuries, the Syrian cities of Aleppo and Damascus were famous for their enamelled and gilded glass. Because of its white sand, Syria had been a major glass-producing area since the Roman period, but this decorative technique of applying gold and colors to the surface of blown vessels was popular mainly during the thirteenth and fourteenth centuries. Many surviving vessels bear inscriptions giving the names or titles of rulers, and others depict activities popular in court circles, such as hunting and drinking.

Although it has no inscription identifying its owner, the imagery on this vessel connects it with courtly taste. On it are depicted birds in an abbreviated landscape setting. Most dramatic is the attack on a duck by a bird of prey, perhaps a falcon. Hunting with falcons was a favorite pastime of Near Eastern rulers and metalwork and ceramics made in Syria during the thirteenth and fourteenth centuries often show similar scenes. This vignette, repeated on both sides of the vessel, occurs near a body of water represented by a blue band, and a small red cloud, symbolizing the sky, is placed above the attacker's head. The remaining birds, arranged in three rows, may have been part of a royal menagerie. Exotic birds and animals were often kept in palaces for the amusement of rulers and their courts. Here the birds include the hoopoe, traditionally associated with royalty in the Near East, and the pheasant, an emblem of rank in China.

Syrian glass was highly esteemed not only among Near Eastern rulers but also in Europe, where fragments have been excavated at various sites and several whole vessels have been preserved in church treasuries or private collections. In Europe special leather cases were often made to protect these delicate objects. It is believed that Syrian enamelled glass first stimulated the glass-blowers at Murano near Venice to decorate vessels in a similar manner.

180

P. S.

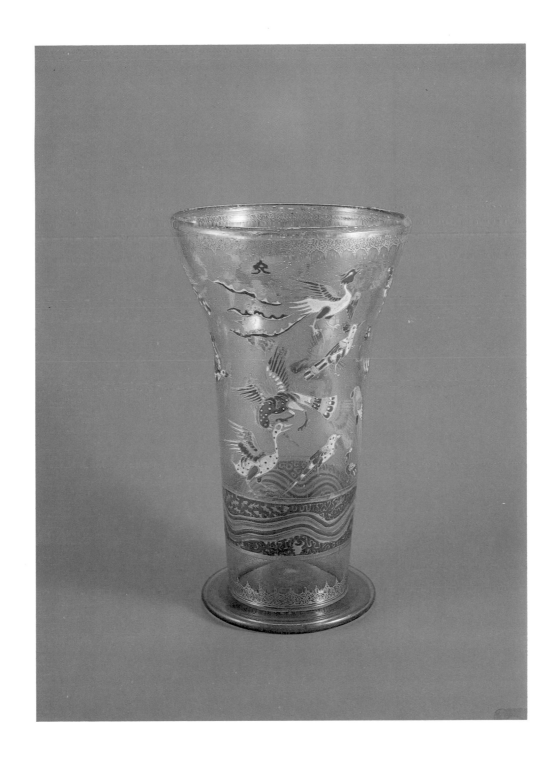

181

SYRIAN

Lamp

Ca. 1360
Enamelled and gilded glass
34 cm. high (13 3/8 in.)
Inventory no. 1060

Lamps hanging from chains were used to illuminate the interiors of Islamic religious buildings. Particularly splendid was a series of enamelled and gilded glass lamps made for the buildings of Damascus and Cairo during the thirteenth and fourteenth centuries. This example bears inscriptions identifying the patron for whom it was made: Sultan al-Nasir Hasan, son of Nasir al-din Muhammad, who ruled between 1347 and 1351 and again between 1354 and 1362. During his second reign, Sultan Hasan ordered the construction of a religious complex containing a congregational mosque, religious schools, and his own mausoleum. It is probable that this lamp was made for use in that complex.

Sultan Hasan's name and titles appear in large letters which surround the zone of the lamp bearing six handles for the attachment of chains. His personal emblem was an abbreviated version of his titles surrounded by a circular frame and this device appears on both the neck and lower portion of this lamp. The lamp's upper zone is dominated, however, by a Koranic verse, Sura 24:35, often inscribed on lamps:

> God is the Light of the heavens and the earth;
> the likeness of His Light is as a niche
> wherein is a lamp
> the lamp in a glass,
> the glass as it were a glittering star.

When this lamp was in use, hanging suspended in the vast space of Sultan Hasan's mosque or mausoleum, it too must have resembled a star in the night sky and its light must have illuminated the titles of Sultan Hasan, reminding all viewers of his pious benefactions.

182

P. S.

183

TURKISH, IZNIK

Plate

Ca. 1575
Alkaline glazed ceramic, underglaze
   painted
30 cm. in diameter (11 3/4 in.)
Inventory no. 2243

This plate combines a shape of Chinese origin with painted decoration similar to that used on many architectural tiles produced in Iznik during the latter decades of the sixteenth century. The Chinese model for this shape, a shallow bowl with a foliated rim, probably dates from the early fifteenth century. Customarily, the rims of such Chinese vessels had a painted design of waves and foam while the center was decorated with clusters of grapes and vine leaves or other foliage patterns. Some Turkish bowls of the early sixteenth century copy not only the shape but also the decoration of the Chinese examples. More common, however, is the approach taken here, in which a stylized reminiscence of the Chinese rim decoration is combined with a new central design taken from the Turkish repertoire. Here, the foliage mingles naturalistic and fanciful elements. A rosebush springs from the lower rim and grows outward and upward, bearing both buds and opened blossoms. In addition to this another vegetal system arising from the same point carries large composite blossoms on its very slender stalks. These blossoms, deriving from Chinese depictions of the lotus, dominate the design of this bowl. Particularly unusual are the outer pair, apparently cut by the edge of the rim, from which spring lance-shaped leaves with blossoms.

The structure of this design is very reminiscent of patterns used in architectural tiles, where often the design was repeated in neighboring panels so that elements falling on the border would be completed in the next unit. Similarities in design between ceramic vessels and architectural tiles are probably the result of their production in the same workshops. Parallels in the design of this piece with tiles from the mosque of Sultan Selim in Edirne, completed in 1575, suggest that this bowl was produced in the 1570s.

P. S.

185

TURKISH, IZNIK(?)

Tiles

Ca. 1580
Alkaline glazed ceramic, underglaze
  painted
96.5 x 24 cm. each (38 x 9 1/2 in.)
Inventory no. 111

During the sixteenth and seventeenth centuries, buildings erected by members of the Ottoman aristocracy were often decorated with revetments of underglaze painted tiles. The greatest center for their production appears to have been the Anatolian city of Iznik. This series of tiles showing tulips and hyacinths below a blossoming fruit tree resembles those still *in situ* in various buildings of the late sixteenth and early seventeenth centuries. Customarily, these compositions of flowering trees and plants are enclosed within an archlike frame, and the ensemble is perhaps intended to recall the view of a garden through an open window. Often these landscape views were not placed side by side as they are here, but were rather separated by panels bearing other designs. As buildings fell into disrepair, tiles were often removed and used again in other structures. The tile panels shown here may have had a similar origin.

Given the wide appeal of the garden theme in Islamic art, it is not surprising that similar groups of tiles are known from both religious and secular monuments. A complex version of this theme is found in the Rustem Pasa mosque, completed around 1564, both used on the porch and the pulpit or *minbar*. Even closer in style to these panels are several in various rooms of the Topkapi Sarayi Palace, residence of the Ottoman Sultans from the fifteenth to eighteenth centuries. A bath built there for Selim II, who ruled from 1566 to 1574, is decorated with tile groups of trees and flowers in which dots are used to embellish both tree trunks and flower petals, as they are here. Also related is the painted decoration of a pleasure pavilion or Kiosk built by Murad III in 1578 within the Harem of the same palace, and a simplified version of the flowering tree is used in the tiles of a mosque built by Ahmet I (1603–17). These comparisons suggest a late sixteenth-century date for the composition in these tiles. More tiles from this same series are now in the University Museum, Philadelphia.

186

P. S.

187

TURKISH, IZNIK

Tankard

Ca. 1590
Alkaline glazed ceramic, underglaze
   painted
30 cm. high (11 3/4 in.)
Inventory no. 834

Ceramics produced in Turkey during the sixteenth and seventeenth centuries reflect the crosscurrents of taste created by trade. This vessel, although decorated in a Turkish style, has a shape of European inspiration. Cast metal drinking vessels may have furnished the model for this tankard's shape, with its flat angular handle. During the sixteenth century, a sizeable population of European merchants and diplomats lived in Pera, located across the Golden Horn from the Ottoman capital, Constantinople. This tankard may have been made for the use of that European community, or even for export to Europe. The floral decoration on it, however, links it with a large body of Ottoman ceramics produced in Iznik. It is particularly notable for the pastel tones of green, lavender, and blue used in the underglaze pigments. This distinctive palette was once thought to characterize ceramics produced in Damascus, but it is more probable that such vessels were made in Iznik along with the more familiar variety executed in blue, green, and red (see page 187). Some vessels using this color scheme may have been produced during the middle decades of the sixteenth century, but this example has affinities with polychrome vessels produced in the last decades of that century. Characteristic for that period is the naturalistic disposition of the vegetation, which here springs from a series of points along the vessel's base. This color scheme was not used for architectural tiles, but the loose arrangement of the foliage seen here has also been used on tiles decorating the mosque of Ahmet I, built between 1609 and 1617.

P. S.

189

The
Far Eastern
Collection

CHINESE

Vase

Qing dynasty, Kang Xi period,
    1662–1722
Hard-paste porcelain with red-rust
    enamel
26.6 cm. high (10 1/2 in.)
Inventory no. 1002

This cylindrical Qing vase, like the deep plate on page 195, is probably from the reign of the emperor Kang Xi, and dates from the late seventeenth or early eighteenth century. The vivid rust-red colored enamelled ground is quite unusual for this period, although red was often used with other colors against a light ground. The design, done in reserve (that is, with a red glaze surrounding areas in which the white of the original clay is revealed), is a stylized floral motif in five registers. The pattern is regular within each band, but each band is unique.

The rust color was produced by a technique developed in the Netherlands in the mid-seventeenth century in which gold was used in the glaze. This technique was imported into China by European traders, and rapidly became very popular. The delicate design is one of the hallmarks of the art of this refined age, and its precise, graceful curves reflect the continued Chinese interest in calligraphy, rhythm, line, and abstract pattern.

192

193

CHINESE

Famille Verte Deep Plate

Qing dynasty, Kang Xi period,
   1662–1722
Polychromed hard-paste porcelain
36.3 cm. in diameter (14 1/4 in.)
Inventory no. 961

Calouste Gulbenkian was, like many collectors of the teens and twenties, most fond of the later Chinese porcelains of the Ming and Qing dynasties, rather than the earlier Han, Tang, and Song that have recently attracted scholarly attention. This deep plate from the Qing dynasty is among many *famille rose* and *famille verte* pieces in his collection. Just as in Western art he was attracted to the Baroque, with its rich, elaborate decorations and highly finished style, so also in Eastern art he chose the delicate, complexly glazed porcelains of the seventeenth and eighteenth centuries.

This plate was probably made in the reign of Kang Xi (1662–1722). It is painted in *famille verte* enamels on a white ground. (*Famille verte* is the term assigned by the original French scholars to a class of porcelains from this period containing a vivid green color.) The detailed decorations are of mythological animals and flowers. The two creatures in the central disc are the phoenix, or *Feng Huang* (above) and the *Qi Lin,* or Chinese unicorn (below). These animals have many symbolic and traditional associations. The *Qi Lin* is an emblem of Perfect Good, while the phoenix, or sun-bird, is related to Indian mythology. Together with a dragon and a tortoise they are the *Si Shen,* the Four Supernatural Creatures who guard or represent the four quadrants of the world. These animal deities have an ancient history in Chinese art and literature, predating Buddhism and going back to the second millenium B.C. They thus bear a totemistic meaning as sacred emblems, and, in the relatively late art of the Qing dynasty, they would also have carried associations of guardianship, venerability, tradition, and, naturally, luck.

Pairs of the Four Creatures were often portrayed together, as here. The Chinese names for the phoenix and unicorn include the words "male" and "female"; the animals thus represent the sexes, the seasons, the points of the compass—in short, in the classical Chinese world view, they are images of the divisions of the universe.

Surrounding the central disc are panels containing other fanciful animals and flowers. These exotic beasts appear to be inventions of the artist. The great intricacy of the design, the bright colors, and the technical polish of the execution are all characteristics of the magnificent porcelain of the time.

195

CHINESE

Two Famille Rose Vases

Qing dynasty, Yong Zheng or
  Qian Long period, 1723–95
Polychromed hard-paste porcelain
132 cm. high each (52 in.)
Inventory no. 344A/B

This pair of covered vases dates from the Qing dynasty, most likely from the reign of Yong Zheng (1723–35) or that of Qian Long (1736–95). During this period ceramics known as *famille rose*, enamelled in soft colors and distinguished by a delicate pink tint, were popular; the fine workmanship characteristic of the style can be seen here. The decoration, in predominantly pink, green, and blue tones, with touches of yellow and black on a white ground, shows exotic birds, perhaps phoenixes, standing among peonies (traditional symbols of longevity or abundance), bamboo, and other flowers. The rims have floral scrolls. The finials on the lids are the famous guardian lions, or dogs of *Fo*, symbols of Imperial China. Dogs of *Fo* were a particularly popular image under the rule of the powerful Qing emperors.

Under these emperors, the great kilns at Jing De Zhen were rebuilt, and porcelains for export to Europe were made in large numbers. As China came into more contact with the West through trade, changes in taste began to appear both in the ceramics made for export and those created for the Chinese aristocracy as well. The earlier purism and austerity of the blue and white Ming ware gave way to the *précieux* sensibility seen in these exquisite vases.

Chinese porcelain of the virtuosity displayed in these pages was the principal influence upon European pottery painters and makers. In the eighteenth century, such vases and plates began to appear in the West, and were there considered the very model of the potter's art. The European vogue for *chinoiserie* was widespread, and stemmed directly from the Oriental *famille verte* and *famille rose* porcelains. Subtlety and refinement were the hallmarks of these wares, with their extreme fragility, graceful shapes, and matchless brushwork.

CHINESE

Vessel

Qing dynasty, Qian Long period,
  1736–95
Brown onyx
15 cm. high (5 7/8 ins.)
Inventory no. 109

This cylindrical vase or decorative brush-holder, made of brown onyx, is from the great age of jade carving, the reign of the emperor Qian Long (1736–95) in the Qing dynasty. Its elaborate design and fine craftsmanship indicate that it was a luxury item, carved in the manner of a scholar's brush-holder, but not necessarily used for that pedestrian purpose. At the time, a wide variety of objects for the scholar's desk was made from jade and other precious hard stones. These included water bowls for rinsing brushes, brush rests, boxes, ink beds, and paperweights made from jade, onyx, chalcedony, lapis lazuli, rock crystal, or rose quartz.

The piece is carved in high and low relief and openwork, in the form of a tree trunk covered with fungi. The twisting stem to the right serves as a handle. As a whole, it seems to be in the midst of a process of organic growth and change. Nature is the major source of motifs in Qing jade, and vessels such as this one are often to be found in the form of a cloud-wreathed cliff, a flower such as the lotus, or an animal. Jades of the Qing dynasty show a particularly high level of technical skill—note here the brilliant gloss of the finish and the minute details—and often have extremely intricate designs.

Although jade carving has an ancient tradition in China, it reached its highest point during the reign of Qian Long, who was a great patron and collector. Under him, the vogue arose for elaborate pieces such as this one; they were furnishings in the house of any scholar or high official of the court, signs of refinement and luxury in imitation of the Imperial taste. Naturalism was part of this vogue, and together with the increased skill of the artists came a virtuosity and flair that have not been equalled. As objects of *virtu*, they were prized for their ornamental grace, exotic forms, and skillful manipulation of the difficult medium. This piece is almost grotesque in its naturalism, evident in the worm holes cut into the bark of the stump and in the gnarled branches. The fungi are symbols of longevity and therefore of good luck.

The ornate and fanciful quality of these jades lends them a certain charm, but they are not always compelling as works of art. Like the ceramics of this period, they may lose in power what they gain in grace and elegance. This vase, however, strikes a fine balance between the bizarre and the merely decorative.

199

JITOKUSAI GYOKUZAN

Active late eighteenth century

Left: *Three-case Inro*

Signed
Edo period, late eighteenth century
Lacquer with mother-of-pearl
8.5 cm. high (3 3/8 in.)
Inventory no. 1329

HARA YOYUSAI

b. Edo, 1772
d. Edo(?), 1845

Right: *Four-case Inro*

Edo period, late eighteenth century
Lacquer
7.7 cm. high (3 in.)
Inventory no. 1364

Japanese decorative arts, particularly the miniature objects known as *inro* (medicine cases) and *netsuke* (small, finely carved wooden or ivory sculptures, sometimes used as buttons), are famous for their technical virtuosity. Lacquer work is a painstaking matter of multiple layers of varnish, built up on a wooden base, and painted and polished with extreme care and patience. With each added layer a metallic or colored powder may be applied, or metal foils or thin pieces of iridescent shell embedded, giving the whole a precious appearance. Like the color woodcuts, the textiles, and the other decorative arts of Japan, fine lacquer work displays the essence of the Zen-influenced Japanese aesthetic: a taste for purified, elegant design; a love of the images of nature refined and formalized; a delight in rich and subtle colors and textures and exotic materials; and a passion for detail. The difficulty of the lacquer medium, its fragility and delicacy, appealed strongly to the Japanese sensibility, and provided the craftsman with an opportunity to show his technical skill.

The lacquer technique came originally from China, and is mentioned in Japanese texts as early as the Koan period (392–291 B.C.). Though it existed for many generations, it reached its apogee in the seventeenth and eighteenth centuries, when it was used to decorate both religious and secular items: furniture, dishes, screens, and small objects such as pipes, combs, and *inro. Inro* are small boxes, usually no more than three or four inches long, having several compartments. They were hung from the sash of a robe by a silk cord and were used to carry powdered medicines, seals, or other things. They were one of the rare forms of jewelry in Japanese costume and were worn by noblemen, Samurai, and merchants, both ceremonially and for utilitarian purposes.

The two *inro* we see here are exceptional examples of the miniaturist's art. The piece on the left, by Jitokusai Gyokuzan, shows a black lacquer snake with finely incised scales set into a ground made of mother-of-pearl chips. It combines the richness of luxurious materials and minute, exact detail with purity of a simple design. This use of contrasting aesthetics is known as *in-yo*, and comes from Chinese tradition. It is one of the basic principles of Japanese art, and is brilliantly rendered here, in the form of a small ornament or trinket.

The box on the right, done in incised and painted vermilion lacquer with colored overlays and inlaid with mother-of-pearl and green ivory, is signed by Yoyusai, one of the foremost lacquer artists of the height of the Edo period. The vivid colors are typical of the art of this period, which for the first time broke away from the Chinese-inspired tradition of monochromatic art. Brightly colored works of art with prosaic, naturalistic scenes, such as this one of a squirrel on a vine, exemplify Japanese taste at its greatest flowering.

NISHIMURA SHIGENOBU

Active 1730–40

Komachi Waving Goodbye to a Lover

Signed
Ca. 1730–40
Colored inks and lacquer on paper, *urushi-e*
31 x 14 cm. (12 3/16 x 5 1/2 in.)
Inventory no. 1957

Shigenobu's two-color (*urushi-e*) print of a courtesan is a prime example of early color printing during the height of the Tokugawa Shogunate in Japan. Japan in the eighteenth century was a closed society whose art had for centuries been the province of the aristocracy; artistic styles had been confined to a few highly regulated schools, and were extremely formulaic and traditional. Toward the middle of the century a group of artists began to break away from the formal schools and to develop a new style of their own. These artists worked in the color woodcut medium because it was inexpensive and popular, producing prints designed for the middle class and showing, in contrast to the art of the great schools, scenes of everyday life of geishas, Kabuki actors, crowded streets, landscapes, cityscapes, and still lifes—in short, what we would call genre subjects, similar to those painted for the bourgeoisie of the Netherlands a century earlier. Because these were considered gay and frivolous topics, the prints were called *ukiyo-e*, pictures from the floating (ephemeral) world. As the genre developed and the prints became popular, the medium and technique were refined, so that broadsheets from the shops of the masters became exemplars of the printer's art, displaying an extraordinary range of subtle colors and metallic tones and great finesse and delicacy of execution. Little is known about Shigenobu, who seems to have worked only for a short time. His prints are made from two woodblocks: on the first, the image is drawn in strong, angular black lines; on the second, a colored ink is applied separately. This was an early stage of *ukiyo-e*, in which color printing was still very limited technically; here the artist has used overlapping areas of black and yellow to create soft shades and textures.

The portrayal of beautiful women was one of the major topics of *ukiyo-e* prints. Like the other artists who drew geishas and courtesans, Shigenobu is here creating an ideal image of grace: hence Komachi's swaying posture and the fluid ripple of her robes. The long, heavy black line of her hair and shoulder is set for emphasis against the flat, geometric background of a screen, while her face and the stylized gesture of her hand are framed by the blossoms of a flowering tree.

The prints of Shigenobu are particularly rare. His work is perhaps less subtle than that of later artists like Utamaro (see following page), having few of the open, blank spaces that give much Japanese art its poetic quality. Instead, he fills his pictures with rich patterns that have great abstract power. Especially beautiful in this print is the wonderfully detailed kimono, brocaded with so many fruits, flowers, and designs that it seems to have a life of its own. Despite the greatly restricted means available to him, Shigenobu has delicately evoked the worldly beauty and luxury of a courtesan's life in the "floating world."

203

KITAGAWA UTAMARO

b. Place unknown, 1753
d. Edo (Tokyo), 1806

Red Dragonfly and Locust on Bamboo Fence

Signed
Page from "A Picture Book of
   Selected Insects"
1788 (first edition)
Colored inks on paper
Double page; each page: 27 x 16.5
   cm. (10 5/8 x 6 1/2 in.)
Inventory no. 2390

Utamaro is one of the true masters of *ukiyo-e* style. The *Book of Insects* consists of fifteen color woodcuts, each a picture of flowers, insects, and sometimes small reptiles, such as snakes and lizards. Each plate is decorated with a poem, written in the graceful, stylized *hiragana* script. These poems, known as *kyōka*, or "mad verses," are often humorous or ribald. The prints are remarkable for their almost scientific accuracy, and even more for their grace, purity, and refinement.

Utamaro was probably familiar with the European books and studies of plants and insects that had become popular in the eighteenth century. He has brought a similar quality of scientific observation to his own illustrations. However, Japanese art has traditionally been deeply concerned with the expression of nature. The veneration of nature amounts to a religious sense, and indeed is linked to Zen Buddhism. Utamaro, dedicating an entire book to the study of insects, has expressed this veneration in all its variety. The perfectly rendered detail on this page reflects his passionate love for the particulars of the visible world.

赤蜻蛉

志のふゝり多くも
それ赤蜻蛉
とのあるひは
瘦ひこけても
　　　　朱楽菅江

露をり
そよきみをそいろこ
のいろ飛のくて
きみをそいろこ
　　　　軒端杉丸

いきこ

Sources for the Text

Introduction (pp. 7–11). José de Azeredo Perdigão, *Calouste Gulbenkian: Collector*. Lisbon, 1969; Edward Lucie-Smith, " 'Mr. Five Percent' Amassed Power Along With Beauty," *Smithsonian Magazine*. 11:42–52, pp. 42–50; Frank Nicolaus, "Der Wahre Reichtum des Milliärdars," *Art: Das Kunstmagazin*. 1:42–52.

Page 16. John Walker and I. E. S. Edwards, *Egyptian Sculpture from the Gulbenkian Collection*. National Gallery of Art, Washington, 1949.

18. Sidney Smith and I. E. S. Edwards, *Ancient Egyptian Sculpture Lent by C.S. Gulbenkian, Esq.* The British Museum, London, 1937.

20. John A. Wilson, *The Culture of Ancient Egypt*. Chicago and London, 1951.

22. Walker and Edwards, *Egyptian Sculpture*.

24. Ibid.

26. Smith and Edwards, *Ancient Egyptian Sculpture*.

28. Ibid.

30. George Steindorff and Keith C. Seele, *When Egypt Ruled the East*. 2nd ed., Chicago and London, 1957.

32. Walker and Edwards, *Egyptian Sculpture*.

36. J. D. Beazley, *Attic Red Figure Vase-Painters*. 2nd ed., Oxford, 1963.

38. Robert Branner, *Manuscript Painting in Paris During the Reign of Saint Louis: A Study of Styles* (California Studies in the History of Art). Berkeley, Los Angeles, and London, 1977.

40. Joseph Natanson, *Gothic Ivories of the 13th and 14th Centuries*. London, 1951.

42. Otto H. Förster, *Stefan Lochner, ein Maler zu Köln*. 3rd ed., Munich, 1948.

44. Martin Davies, *Rogier van der Weyden: An Essay with a Critical Catalogue of Paintings Assigned to Him and to Robert Campin*. New York, 1972.

46. John L. Ward, "A Proposed Reconstruction of an Altarpiece by Rogier van der Weyden," *Art Bulletin*. 53:27–35.

48. Max J. Friedländer, *Dieric Bouts and Joos van Ghent, Early Netherlandish Painting*. Vol. 3 (Trans. Heinz Norden), Leyden and Brussels, 1968.

50. G. F. Hill, *Pisanello*. London and New York, 1905.

52. John Pope-Hennessy, *Italian Renaissance Sculpture* (An Introduction to Italian Sculpture, Part II). London and New York, 1971.

54. John Pope-Hennessy, *Luca della Robbia*. Ithaca, 1980.

56. S. J. Freedberg, *Painting of the High Renaissance in Rome and Florence*. 2 vols., Cambridge, Massachusetts, 1961.

58. Ibid.

60. Luigi Coletti, *Cima da Conegliano*. Venice, 1959.

62. Jan Lauts, *Carpaccio: Paintings and Drawings*. (Trans. Erica Millman and Marguerite Kay), London, 1962.

64. Frederick Hartt, *Giulio Romano*. 2 vols., New Haven, 1958.

66. Max J. Friedländer, *Jan Gossaert and Bernart van Orley, Early Netherlandish Painting*. Vol. 8 (trans. Heinz Norden), Leyden and Brussels, 1972.

68. Seymour Slive, *Frans Hals*. (National Gallery of Art Kress Foundation Studies in the History of European Art). 3 vols., London, 1970–74.

70. Jakob Rosenberg. *Rembrandt, Life and Work*. Rev. ed., London, 1964.

72. A. Bredius, *Rembrandt: The Complete Edition of the Paintings*. Rev. ed., London, 1971.

74. Leo van Puyvelde, *Rubens*. Brussels, 1964.

76. Julius S. Held, *The Oil Sketches of Peter Paul Rubens: A Critical Catalogue*. 2 vols., Princeton, 1980.

78. Leo van Puyvelde, *Van Dyck*. Brussels and Amsterdam, 1950.

80. G. Wildenstein, *Lancret*. Paris, 1924.

82. Alexandre Ananoff and Daniel Wildenstein, *François Boucher*. Lausanne and Paris, 1976.

84. Maurice Block, *François Boucher and the Beauvais Tapestries*. Boston and New York, 1933.

85. Adolph S. Cavallo, *Tapestries of Europe and of Colonial Peru in the Museum of Fine Arts, Boston*. 2 vols., Boston, 1967.

86. F. J. B. Watson, *Louis XVI Furniture*. London, 1960.

90. Georges Wildenstein, *The Paintings of Fragonard: Complete Edition*. (Trans. C. W. Chilton and A. L. Kitson), London, 1960.

94. Pierre de Nolhac, *Hubert Robert, 1733–1808*. Paris, 1910.

96. Albert Besnard, *La Tour: La Vie et l'oeuvre de l'artiste, Catalogue critique*, Paris, 1928.

98. Ellis Waterhouse, *Gainsborough*. London, 1958.

100. Humphrey Ward and W. Roberts, *Romney: A Biographical and Critical Essay with a Catalogue Raisonné of His Works*. 2 vols., London, 1904.

102. Kenneth Garlick, *Sir Thomas Lawrence*. (English Master Painters), London, 1954.

104. H. H. Arnason, *The Sculpture of Houdon*. London, 1975.

106. Ibid.

108. Antonio Morassi, *L'Opera completa di Antonio e Francesco Guardi*. Venice, 1973.

110. Ibid.

112. A. J. Finberg, *The Life of J. M. W. Turner, R. A.* Second rev. ed., London, 1961.

114. Ibid.

116. Robert L. Herbert, *Barbizon Revisited*. New York, 1962.

118. Ibid.

120. Ibid.

122. Alfred Robaut, *L'Oeuvre de Corot: Catalogue Raisonné et illustré*. 4 vols., Paris, 1965.

124. Germain Bazin, *Corot*. Paris, 1973.

126. Robaut, *L'Oeuvre de Corot*.

128. Edward Lucie Smith, *Fantin Latour*. Oxford, 1977.

130. G. Jean-Aubry and Robert Schmit, *Eugène Boudin*. (Trans. Caroline Tisdall), Greenwich, Connecticut, 1968.

132. Denis Rouart and Daniel Wildenstein, *Edouard Manet: Catalogue raisonné*. Vol. 1, Lausanne and Paris, 1975.

134. Ibid.

136. P. A. Lemoisne, *Degas et son oeuvre*. 4 vols., Paris, 1946.

138. Theodore Reff, "Pictures within Pictures," *Degas: The Artist's Mind*. New York, 1976.

140. Adelyn Dohme Breeskin, *Mary Cassatt, A Catalogue Raisonné of the Oils, Pastels, Watercolors, and Drawings*. Washington, 1970.

142. François Daulte, *Auguste Renoir: Catalogue raisonné de l'oeuvre peint*. Vol. 1, Lausanne, 1971.

144. William C. Seitz, *Claude Monet*. New York, n.d.

146. Ibid.

148. Albert E. Elsen, *Rodin*. New York, 1963.

150. Martin Harrison and Bill Walters, *Burne-Jones*. London, 1973.

164. *The Koran Interpreted*. (Trans. A. J. Arberry), New York, 1964. Quotations from the Koran appearing in the text are from Vol. 2, pp. 352 and 188 respectively.

166. Ralph Pindar-Wilson and William Watson, "An Inscribed Jade Cup from Samarqand," *British Museum Quarterly*. Vol. 23, 1960–61, pp. 19–22.

168. Jahangir, *The Tuzuk-i Jahangiri*. (Trans. Rogers, ed. Beveridge), 2nd ed., Delhi, Vol. 1, p. 146.

170. Sa'di, *The Bustan: Morals Pointed and Tales Adorned*. (Trans. G. M. Wickens), Toronto, 1974, p. 102.

176. May H. Beattie, *Carpets of Central Persia*, 1976, pp. 14–18, 26–27.

182. *The Koran Interpreted*. Vol. 2, pp. 50–51.

192. R. L. Hobson, *The Later Ceramic Wares of China*, London, 1975.

194. William Cohn, "The Deities of the Four Cardinal Points in Chinese Art," *Transactions of the Oriental Ceramic Society*. London, vol. 8, 1940; W. B. Honey, *Guide to the Later Chinese Porcelain*. Victoria and Albert Museum, London, 1927.

196. Hobson, *The Later Ceramic Wares of China*.

198. S. Howard Hansford, "Jade and Jade Carvings in the Ch'ing Dynasty," *Transactions of the Oriental Ceramic Society*. London, Vol. 35, 1963–64.

200. Melvin and Betty Jahss, *Inro and Other Miniature Forms of Japanese Lacquer Art*. Rutland, Vermont, 1976.

202. J. Hillier, *Utamaro: Colour Prints and Paintings*. 2nd ed., New York, 1979.

204. Richard Lane, *Images from the Floating World: The Japanese Print*. New York, 1978.

Index of Artists